He Told Me

Christopher L. Price

Copyright © 2015 Christopher L. Price

All rights reserved. No part of this book may be reproduced or transmitted in any form or by any means, electronically or mechanically, including photocopying, recording, or by any information storage or retrieval system, without the permission in writing from the author.

Printed and bound in the United States of America

International Standard Book Number: 978-0-9829776-4-4

Foreword

After much thought and prayer, I finally decided to write *He told Me*, the sequel to my first memoir, *I Stood Alone*. My goal in writing *He Told Me* was simply to relate the truth of my experiences. I took great care to share those truths in a manner consistent with the verity of those experiences (whether painful or joyful), while also being mindful of my family's and friends' feelings regarding those experiences.

I Stood Alone related the experiences of a young man who had persevered in spite of the enormity of his circumstances with the judicial and penal systems; *He Told Me* chronicles the experiences of that same young man post his incarceration. While *I Stood Alone* casually touched upon my familial relationships, *He Told Me* delves into my relationship with my family and friends in a far more intimate manner.

It is because of the depth of intimacy of my relationships that I was hesitant to relate my experiences. However, as I examined my relationships and experiences, I understood that someone, some reader, may gain strength and a purpose for existing through the telling of my story. And, so, it was with the conviction of the Spirit that I present *He Told Me*.

Acknowledgements

I humbly thank God for blessing me with the strength and tenacity to write this piece. Without the Creator's grace, I would not have had the vision or desire to complete the work.

I also acknowledge ex-offenders everywhere. Our roads are seldom easy; I pray strength and tenacity on your journey.

Lastly, I thank God for my parents. Our journey together has not been replete of its struggles, yet I have always thanked the Creator for blessing me with you. I love you, wholly.

Dedication

This book is dedicated to Sean Christopher Rowland, Sr. (1974-2019); a friend to the end.

He Told Me

Yes, I'd like to apply for a job...
Uh, yeah, but I served my time
I can't even flip burgers?
But I'm two semesters from graduating...
From college.

He told me, "Man, it's rough out here."

Hi, can I use your car to take
Mother to the doctor?
I have my license...
But it's for my grandmother
I'm sorry I asked.

He told me, "Man, people done changed."

Huh?
I can't use a stamp
To write my friend a letter
He locked up
Oh, you can't afford it...
It's 34 cents.

He told me, "Man, they for they selves out here."

You say you want
Me to put your car
In my name?
You ain't got no license
No insurance...
They stop u, it's on me.
I'm on parole.
You mad?

He told me, "Man, they don't care about you."

So what, so you just yell
At people? What did
Life do to you? Where
Did the sweetness go? Were
You always like this? Did you
Pull a fast one on me? Who
Are you?

He told me, "Man, home ain't home no mo'."

Life is fraught with experiences: some pleasant; others are trying and difficult to overcome. The Holy Spirit encourages us to continue moving forward, even in the face of adversity. We must not allow life and the hardships of living to stop us from fulfilling the Creator's will...

Table of Contents

Foreword 3
Acknowledgements 4
Chapter Two 34
Chapter Three 43
Chapter Four 60
Chapter Five 74
Chapter Six 84
Chapter Seven 95
Chapter Eight 103
Chapter Nine 119
Chapter Ten 132
Chapter Eleven 143
Chapter Twelve 166
Chapter Thirteen 179
Chapter Fourteen 206
Chapter Fifteen 213
Chapter Sixteen 218
Chapter Seventeen 243
Chapter Eighteen 247
Chapter Nineteen 257
Chapter Twenty 270

Chapter One

The brisk, cool, December air wrapped itself around me, piercing my thin, gray sweat-suit. I looked across the vast parking lot in search of my father. Through squinted eyes, I peered over the rows and rows of vehicles until I saw a dark figure standing beside a white truck. *That had to be him. The truck looked exactly as the one in the pictures.* I cautiously walked in the direction of the truck, slowly at first and then with more determination. I desperately wanted to escape the chill of the wind, though, more importantly, I needed to separate myself from the gloomy fortress behind me.

For six and a half years Lima Correctional Institution had been my home, of sorts. I still vividly remembered the day that my cousin, Booger, and I were bound together by chains and transported there; with measured steps, we pigeon-walked down the stairs of the bus and into the over-sized kitchen of the institution. The stench of bug spray greeted us, nearly suffocating the air from our lungs. Trails of mice droppings were visible along the brick walls and beneath the steel prepping tables. As I looked around at the frightened, young faces of the inmates around me, I steeled myself for the horrors to come.

"Welcome to the Lima Correctional Institution, your new fucking home!" A large, red-faced, CO (correctional officer) barked. The CO surveyed his newest residents, peering into each of our eyes with his ice-blue radars. "For whatever fucking reason, the State has determined that you pieces of shit should be reprimanded to my custody for however long I deem necessary!"

I looked at Booger to see how he was handling the CO's rants. As usual, Booger was as cool as a cucumber. He seemed unaffected by the CO's antics and the horrible condition of the dungeon.

Although I was not at all fazed by the CO's bellowing, I could not stop my mind from thinking of the circumstances that had placed us there:

"Stupid, Black bitch," the White guy yelled.

"Don't put yo mother-fuckin hands on me!" Tookie screamed.

Swoosh! Without warning an orange-reddish color exploded from the rifle.

"Chris, what happened?!"

"I don't know. I think I shot somebody.

"Christopher Price, guilty of the lesser included offense, involuntary manslaughter."

A collage of memories flooded my mind. Despite my valiant attempts, I still could not believe that I had taken someone's life and that I had been incarcerated for a total of seven and a half years.

I forced my mind to focus on the present. As I walked across the parking lot of Lima Correctional Institution, I thought of my friends that I was leaving behind. I would miss them dearly. In the six and a half years that I was caged in Lima, they had become my family. Together we had eaten bland, unappealing meals in the cafeteria; we had worked alongside one another; recreated together; we had experienced the tragedy of the death of one of the correctional center's employees. We had forged bonds that time could not erase, nor could distance separate.

Crossing the black abyss of the tar-paved parking lot to my daddy's truck, my heart was heavy; saddened. I did not why. I searched my mind trying to ascertain the reason for my mood. Could it have been the less-than-warm conversation that I had with my daddy prior to his arrival to the institution, or maybe it was the look of animosity on the CO's face as I smugly exited the institution? Perhaps one, or both, of those events had penetrated my soul somehow, clouding my joy.

My release from the dismal dungeon should have been one of the happiest days of my young life. I was free. The whole world lay ahead of me. The promise of fulfilling dormant dreams should have been fixed firmly in my mind, yet a foreboding enveloped me; a spiritual intuition that something was amiss.

I was two months from my twenty-second birthday when I had entered the walls of the penitentiary. At the time of my release, I was twenty-eight years old; an adult man in many regards, though a vulnerable, innocent child in other ways. Prison had stunted my growth and, strangely, had protected me in ways that I was yet unaware.

As I neared the truck, I could more clearly see my daddy's overstuffed body. His bright, radiant smile glistened beautifully against the backdrop of the gray, dismal skies. With each step that I took, his facial features became clearer. His warm, toasted-brown, skin and soft, amber-colored eyes were more visible. I slowly placed the brown, paper bag on the ground before me. The luggage, of sorts, held six and a half years of my most valued possessions: my photo album and old letters that I had received over the seven and a half years of my confinement.

I walked into his outstretched arms. He held me firmly for a long moment. My frustration with having to wait for him to come to get me dissipated in the warmth of his embrace; the hurt of his scolding words slid from my mind. Slowly, his love for me had begun to pierce the pain-filled walls of the embryonic sac surrounding my heart. I had missed him more than I knew; more than I had allowed myself feel. He kissed me roughly on my cheek before releasing me from his stronghold.

"Son, you are going to freeze out here," he said, standing back, looking at me in my thin jogging suit, "You don't have any long-johns on under that?" He asked, directing his gaze at my clothes.

"No," I smiled, embarrassedly.

"See, y'all don't know how to dress for this Ohio weather. I layer up for this weather." He raised his hooded sweat shirt to reveal, not one, but four or five different shirts beneath the hoodie! "And that ain't all. I got a pair of long-johns under these," he said, pointing to his pants. "And, you see these socks?! These are thermal socks." He raised the leg of his pants, revealing red-topped, gray, wool socks. "This ain't Georgia!" He said, referring to the warm weather of his new home state.

I could not help but to laugh. He was so sincere and passionate about his Eskimo-like wardrobe. It suddenly made sense to me why he had looked as large as a polar bear when I first saw him in the distance. He had on enough clothes and underclothes to keep seven people warm!

My laughter brought him from his tangent. He suddenly realized that I had been standing there shivering against the piercing wind as he shared his latest in winter clothes.

"Oh, I brought a couple guest for you," he motioned with his hand toward the dark, tinted windows of his truck.

Slowly, the front and back passenger doors of the truck began to open. To my surprise and delight, my younger brothers, Jeremiah and Corey, exited the truck. Jeremiah and Corey were my half-brothers: Miah-Miah, as I called Jeremiah, was my maternal half-brother and Corey was my paternal half-brother. I had only seen them once during the time that I was incarcerated. They had grown quite a bit. Both of them were the same height as me, which did not say a lot, considering I only stood at 5'8; though when one considered that I was separated by eleven and twelve years in age from them, the height difference spoke volumes.

I simultaneously gave them both big bear-hugs; separating only to look into their faces and then hugging them once more. Miah-Miah looked more like Mymomme as he aged: his oval-shaped face and features had been inherited from her. Although Corey was not my maternal brother, he could have easily passed for a Randle. His beautiful, dark skin and radiant smile were physical traits in which the Randles wore proudly.

"We had better get in the truck before we catch pneumonia out here!" I laughed as I disengaged from our embrace.

It was cold, with promises of being colder. At the first week of December, we still had several more months of frigid temperatures and mountains of snow to come.

I turned around to look at the fortress one last time before I got into the truck. Six and a half years of absolute confinement. My heart ached for all of the years I had lost; years that I could never get back.

"How have y'all been?" I turned to ask my brothers as they sat comfortably on the back seat of my daddy's truck. I had not been in a civilian vehicle in seven and a half years. It felt strange; nice, but strange.

"I been cool. What about you, little bro?!" Jeremiah asked, laughing. He delighted in being the same height and size as me.

I laughed with him, "I've been cool…glad to get out of there," I said, nodding my head in the direction of the prison.

"Man, I feel you," Jeremiah replied, understandingly.

"How about you, Corey, how have you been?" I asked.

"I'm well," Corey responded through white, even teeth. He had a small gap through his two front teeth, much like my own. I had vowed while I was incarcerated that I would get braces placed on my teeth upon my release from prison. The gap between my teeth was attractive to me when I was younger. It seemed to add character to my boyish face. Now that I was older, it was less appealing to me.

"Cool. How is school?" I asked.

Corey had attended parochial schools his entire life. The quality of his education showed in the manner in which he spoke. His grammar and enunciation were remarkable, especially for an adolescent of his age.

"It's going well," he smiled, shyly.

I continued to chat with my brothers and my daddy about the things that were going on in their lives. Miah-Miah shared with me the news of the birth of his son, Chase. Although Mymmome had already told me that Miah-Miah was a father, the news was still hard for me to believe. It seemed like just a few short years ago I was potty-training Miah-Miah. Now, he was a father, albeit a young one. The years had truly gone by quickly.

Before we drove onto the highway to drive the seventy miles to Toledo, we stopped at a gas station. I jumped out of the truck to assist my daddy with pumping the gas. I was eager to see what the new gas pumps looked liked. I had been told that I would not know how to use them.

While the appearance of the gas pumps was different than those that were used before I was incarcerated, the concept had not changed. One still had to remove the pump from a holster and insert it in the gas tank of the vehicle. The older gas pumps utilized analog numbers to indicate how much gas had been pumped; the newer pumps were digital. No big difference between the old and the new, I surmised.

After we left the gas station, we stopped at McDonald's. I had dreamed about fast food while I was incarcerated. I could not wait until I had the opportunity to eat what I wanted to eat and when I wanted to eat. However, as I stood at the counter waiting for the cashier to take my order, nothing seemed appealing. In the end, I ordered a cup of orange juice and a hash brown, which I had half-eaten.

~~~~

I awakened with a start. My heartbeat quickened. I rose from the seat, quickly looking around myself, trying to gather my bearings. I looked at the dashboard. The clock listed the time as 11:07. I exhaled sharply.

"You all right, son?" My daddy asked.

I half-smiled. "Yeah, I thought it was count-time," I laughed.

For the past seven and a half years, we inmates were counted three times a day to ensure that none of us had escaped. The morning count always began at precisely 10:45 a.m. It would take some time for me to get used to being free.

I looked behind myself. Jeremiah and Corey were sound asleep.

I snuggled back into my seat. I had awakened just as my daddy entered Rossford, a suburb of Toledo, Ohio. Although I was home, I did not feel the warm, welcoming feelings that a person typically associated with being home. Involuntarily, my mind had taken me to the day that my family and I were chased for a block and a half on Maumee Avenue by a gang of angry Whites. I felt the throbbing pain in my arm of being hit with a tire iron by one of the gang members as if it had just happened.

"Son, you know your grandmother was diagnosed with the early onset of Alzheimer's, don't you?" My daddy asked, breaking my reverie.

Mother, as family and friends referred to her, was my paternal grandmother. Her debilitating mental state was not news to me. A few weeks prior, my daddy had mentioned the same grave news. However, I was so enthralled in the events leading to my release that I had not given her mental condition the thought it deserved.

As I sat in the truck, I remembered a visit that I had received from my cousins and Mother a few months earlier. Mother's behavior seemed peculiar. Within fifteen minutes of arriving at the prison for the visit, she announced that she was ready to leave. Her eyes had a distant, faraway look, as though her mind was someplace else. The events of that day suddenly made sense.

"Yes, I remember you telling me a few weeks ago," I replied solemnly.

The thought that Mother had Alzheimer's was frightening. I desperately wanted things to be the same as they were when I had left home seven and a half years ago. In fact, a huge part of me needed to return home to familiar things and familiar people. My own mental health was dependent upon it. Prison had robbed me of the security that so many of us took for granted. In the twinkle of an eye, my entire world was turned upside down. One hour, I was preparing to attend a carnival with my friends and the next hour I was entangled in a vicious fight for my life with a gang of White Supremacists.

Each and every day I had prayed that none of my family members died while I was incarcerated. While I was blessed in that no one had passed away during my prison term, Mother's mental condition was near-death to me. A major part of who she was lied in her memory: her laughter, her stories, her sense of humor, her loving spirit. Without her memory, would she not be merely a shell of her former self?

~~~

The city looked different to me, yet the same. The landscape had aged: tattered streets greeted our entrance into the city; the buildings appeared depressed, as though they had been stripped of their color; old, debilitating homes were replaced with empty lots.

We drove down the familiar, weather-worn streets until we reached Mother's home. The four of us stepped out of the truck. The chilled air quickly greeted us as we placed our feet on the concrete pavement. Mother's home looked exactly as it had when I last saw it; although, it appeared out of place in the crime-ridden area: the small front yard was neatly manicured; green outdoor carpet covered the porch and the driveway; the white aluminum siding of the house shined brightly.

Drugs and gangs had slowly begun to claim the territory thirty years prior. Proof of the assertion was evident in the lavish, steel bars and massive security doors that adorned the windows and the front and rear entrances of Mother's home. As we walked to the side entrance of the house, my eyes caught sight of the heavy-duty chains that bound the porch furniture together—a deterrent against theft.

The driveway, once painted a bright green, was replaced with green, outdoor carpet. My brothers and I stood outside as my daddy unlocked the doors. Stepping into the house, the aroma met us before we had an opportunity to walk into the kitchen. The sweet scent of cakes permeated the air. The fragrance was powerful; albeit welcoming. I had dreamed of coming home to the allurement of Mother's delicious cakes.

Mother turned around for a moment as we entered the kitchen and then continued cooking at the stove.

"Hi, Mother," I greeted softly, smiling.

Mother turned around, again, "Hey, doll. I ain't seen you in awhile."

I smiled broadly as I made my way around the kitchen table to hug her. "I know. It has been awhile," I laughed. In truth, it had been nearly a year since we had last seen one another, but I did not say anything.

"Mother, you know who this is?" My daddy asked her as he pointed at me.

Mother looked at him incredulously, rolled her eyes, ignoring his question.

"Who is he?" My daddy persisted.

"Santa Claus," Mother said, matter-of-factly. She rolled her eyes once more as she turned her head back in the direction of the stove. I laughed involuntarily.

She turned to me, "Chris, you want something to eat?" I laughed, again. Despite being nearly ninety years old and stricken with Alzheimer's, she had not lost any of her spunk, humor, and, apparently, not much of her memory—at least not much of her long term memory.

"No, ma'am, I'm fine. I don't have much of an appetite for some reason."

"No?" She asked with concern.

"Mmm mhm. I don't know why. Maybe it's the excitement of being home."

"Mother, you know Chris just came home from prison, don't you?" My daddy asked.

Again, Mother ignored him. Looking pass my daddy to where Corey stood, "Corey, I didn't see you over there! How you doing? Been a long time since you came by to see me…"

"Hi, Mother," Corey smiled, as he walked over to hug Mother. "I didn't want to interrupt you while you were talking to Chris. Is Autumn here?"

"I think she upstairs," Mother responded in her deep voice.

Moments later, Corey descended the stairs with Autumn. Autumn was my cousin. Her mother and I were first cousins. I had not seen her since she was a child of about four years of age. She was now fifteen. Although she had obviously matured, she was still the pretty, outgoing child that she had been as a young girl. With outstretched arms, she quickly walked to where I stood.

"Hi, Chris!" She said in a flawlessly, beautiful voice.

"Hey, Autumn," I said, smiling, as I greeted her with a hug.

"How you been?" She asked, warmly.

"I've been good…" I laughed.

She looked up at the hat which half-covered my hair.

"Ohh, let me see your hair!"

I slowly took the hat off of my head. I was self-conscious. My hair was a mess. Ordinarily, I would not have been caught dead with my hair looking as it did; however, I had plans.

"Oooh, it's long! Can I braid it, please?!" Autumn asked, excitedly.

I laughed, "You want to braid this nappy stuff?!"

"Ooh, yeah, your hair is the perfect texture for braiding, 'cause the braids stay tight longer!"

"Oh, okay," I laughed. "Maybe after I get it done."

"Done? What you gone do to it?"

"I want to get it cut in a style and permed," I smiled.

While I was incarcerated, I wrote a list of the things that I wanted to do when I returned home. One of the things on the list was to get my hair cut, styled, and relaxed in a style similar to what Anita

Baker had made famous in the 1980s. I knew that such a style on a man was risqué, but I figured it would give me an advantage in the world of modeling. Few African American male models donned long hair. Generally, our hair was closely cropped, giving us little chance for versatility. One of the many things female models had in their favor was their ability to effortlessly change their appearance. Simply by applying make-up and a different hair style, women could drastically alter how they looked. I concluded that it was in my best interest to give myself a different look, which would make me more marketable as a male model.

I had modeled unprofessionally as a teenager and young adult; although, I did not like to model, particularly in fashion shows. I felt uncomfortable walking across a stage as though I was the finest man on earth in front hundreds of people. The act required a bit of narcissism and an affinity for public adulation. I had neither; though, I reasoned that, because I had a felony on my record, jobs would be difficult to acquire. I had to do what I could do to survive. Modeling could prove to be the only way for me to be self-sufficient. If it was the route I had to travel toward self-sufficiency, then runways here I come!

"Oh, I see you! Kinda like a little pimp thing going on! Uhn huh, I see you, cousin!" Autumn laughed.

"Yeah, I guess...," I laughed. I liked Autumn. She had a great personality.

My daddy entered the kitchen from the living room. "Well, son, are you ready to head out to your grandmother's?"

Yes! I thought to myself. My stomach flipped and twisted at the thought of finally seeing Mama.

"Yes," I responded coolly.

Although I had truly looked forward to seeing Mother, my heart was set on seeing Mama, my maternal grandmother. I had missed all of my family members deeply, but I needed to see Mama. My homecoming would not be real until I saw her face and heard her familiar, southern drawl and warm greeting of, "Hey, baby."

It was then that I would know I was home; that all of what I was experiencing was not a dream.

~~~

Mother and Mama only lived a short distance from each other. We arrived in front of Mama's house within seven minutes. I looked at the small, brick house through the window of my daddy's truck. The house looked far smaller than I had remembered. The yard which had seemed humongous to me as a child, was no more than a quaint piece of land.

Wow! Look at that tree! As children, against my grandfather's wishes, my cousins and I used to climb, what appeared to be, a huge oak tree. The tree looked more like a twig in comparison to the way it had looked to me as a child.

Once, when I was about eight years old, my younger cousin, Deandre, was stuck in the tree. I had to climb the tree and assist him down before Allen, our grandfather, came home. If he had caught us in the tree, one of branches would have surely met our behind.

I chuckled to myself at the memory. It was amazing how the world looked so different through the lenses of my adult eyes.

I turned the door knob of the front door and gave it a little push. As I had expected the door was unlocked. It swung open. The swirled, smoke-gray carpet was the first thing that I saw as I stepped into the living room. I turned my head to the right and there she sat. She looked beautiful in a housedress as she lounged on the large, black leather sofa. Her silver hair was cut in a short afro; the soft curls accentuated her round, full cheeks and almond-colored skin wonderfully.

"Hi, Mama," I smiled, broadly.

"Hey, baby," she greeted, warmly, as she twisted and shifted her body on the sofa in an attempt to stand to her feet.

"You don't have to stand," I said as I quickly walked to where she sat.

I squatted down to hug her. She wrapped her arms around me in a warm, firm embrace. She held me there for a long moment, rocking me gently before letting me go. I kissed her ample cheek before I stood up.

"I'm sure glad you home, baby."

"I'm glad to be home, Mama," I smiled as I looked around the house.

"Hey, Andy. How was the drive down there?" Mama asked my daddy.

"It wasn't bad, Ms. Randle. I stopped to pick up Jeremiah and Cory before I headed down there."

The rooms in the house appeared much smaller. Mama had done a little remodeling. Gone was the rust-colored sofa and peach-colored chairs. The newly acquired black leather sofa and chair occupied much of the space in the small room. I looked in the direction of the dining room. The massive oak dining table, china cabinet, and buffet were familiar remnants of the past. The tablecloth and placemats were the only things that had been changed in the room.

"You seen yo' mother, yet?" Mama asked me in her soft, southern tone.

"No, we came here first."

"Oh," She replied, thoughtfully.

Although Mama never intentionally wanted to come between my relationship with Mymomme, she took great pride in knowing that I loved her specially.

"Well, baby, you better go by and see about her. You know how that girl get."

I chuckled at Mama's remark. Mymomme made it no secret that she was possessive of me to the extent in which she was jealous of any relationship that she deemed closer than the one she and I shared.

"I am. I'm going to go to see her after I leave here. I needed to see you, though."

We locked eyes. Words need not explain the love we felt for one another. Although she was not my birth mother, her love for me was akin to the love between a mother and her child.

At the tender young age of eleven, Mama allowed me to reside with Allen and her during Mymomme's substance abuse years. From that time onward, we shared an unbreakable bond.

"Okay. I'm going to go by Mymomme's."

"Okay, baby. I'll see you later on today," Mama said.

Mama and I hugged each other before I stood to leave. Being held in her warm embrace made coming home all the more worthwhile.

~~~

After leaving Mama's, my daddy and I went directly to Mymomme's house. The appearance of her house had not changed much either during the time that I was gone. I walked up the cracked stairs and onto the loose floorboards of the porch to knock on the door. I stood on the porch for several minutes until I knocked again. I thought I had heard a sound from inside the house, so I knocked once more. I placed my ear closer to the door to better hear if someone was inside, however no one came to the door. I knocked one last time before I eventually conceded and left.

I was dismayed. I badly wanted to see Mymomme's smiling face and to touch her smooth, soft skin. Mama held an important place in my heart, though so, too, did Mymomme.

Mymomme was the foundation upon who I was as a person. Despite her personal shortcomings, it was Mymomme who had equipped me with the values of honesty and fairness. She taught me to be strong and independent, to defend myself, and to express my truth in the face of adversity. In many ways, it was Mymomme who provided me with the essential tools of personhood.

I needed to see her. I could not imagine where she could be. She knew I was coming home and that I would have wanted to see her. My heart began to crack. As I turned to exit the porch, I breathed in deeply and slowly exhaled the air from my lungs, trying as best I could to allow the disappointment that I felt to seep from my body, mind, and heart.

~~~

My daddy stopped the truck in front of the salon. I got out of the truck and walked up the few stairs into the beauty shop. No sooner than I had moved beyond the foyer, I heard a loud scream.

"Ahhhhh…" a familiar, high-pitched scream rang loudly.

Monique was an old family friend of the Randle's. She was a gem of a person. At 5'3, she had the spirit of an Amazon warrior, yet the kindness of a nun. Before my incarceration, Monique permed and styled my hair in finger waves to absolute perfection. I would wake early some Saturday and Sunday mornings with hopes of being the first to arrive at her home to get my hair fried and dyed, only to find myself amongst a room full of other persons who had the same objective in mind.

Monique had come a long way since then. She had earned a beautician's license, had won several hair styling contests, and she was well-known throughout the city as an excellent hair stylist.

I lifted my head toward the voice of the woman screaming. I was startled. It had been quite some time since I had heard anyone scream, especially a woman. I smiled bashfully as Monique ran toward me with outstretched arms. Everyone in the small, well-decorated salon turned to look at us. I felt uncomfortable; bashful. I did not like attention.

"Hey, baby!" Monique yelled into my ear as she hugged me with the strength of a grizzly bear.

I smiled broadly, while still trying to compose myself, "Hi, Monique."

Monique held onto for me a quite awhile, rocking me back and forth in a matronly way. Despite the discomfort I felt from everyone looking at us, I allowed her to have her moment. Aside from Monique being a very passionate person, her love of me was fierce. The fervor she displayed was merely an indication of her sincere miss of me. As we separated from our embrace, I saw that tears had cascaded down her chocolate-colored cheeks.

She twirled around like a ballerina toward the patrons and beauticians in the shop, "This is my baby, y'all! I remember when he was a little boy in diapers!" She declared, proudly.

Again, I smiled shyly. All eyes were on us. I did not know what else to do, so I nodded my head in the direction of the people in the beauty shop and thanked Monique.

She was correct. Not only had she been my hair stylist as a young adult, but she had also been an invaluable friend. Our families had emotional ties that began long before my birth. In fact, she was far more than merely a friend to me, she was like a treasured aunt.

~~~

While Monique was excellent at her craft, she was horrible with time management. She attempted to do way too many things at once:

"Can you shampoo her while I bump Tamika's hair…….Hold on, I'ma put you under the dryer in just a sec…where is my chicken……Chile, I'ma take a break to eat……Girl, let me tell you what Nae-Nae said the other day…"

Like a bat fleeing from Hell, Monique would run around the beauty shop trying to do a thousand things. Her multitude of clients would be upset enough to turn Hell upside down as they impatiently waited to be the next person in her chair; however, when Monique finished her work and spun the clients around in the chair to view her masterpiece, all irritation with Monique would fall from their shoulders like water slides from a duck's back.

~~~

I nearly ran to the shampoo station. I myself had never experienced the fiery pits of Hell, though I imagined that it must have felt a lot like what I was undergoing.

My scalp was on fire! Every pore of my head, from the front of my hairline to the nape of my neck, screamed for relief. *"If I can just submerge my entire head in a bucket of cool water I know everything will be all right!"* I thought.

I did not know what I was thinking when I decided to allow Monique to relax my hair. I knew beyond a shadow of a doubt that my scalp would be blistered from ear to ear, front to back, and throughout all the tightly coiled hairs on my head!

I sat miserably in Monique's chair as she used her tools to sway my hair in this direction, then in that direction. With each sway, I felt as though the skin was being ripped from my head. As badly as I wanted to look out the corners of my eyes to see my head, I refused to look anywhere near my head until she was done. I imagined the only thing that would have remained on the top of my head would be a few strands of hair that had somehow managed to avoid the fierceness of the white lava in a jar.

Finally, she swung the chair around for me to face the mirror. I held my eyes tightly closed. I was afraid to see what I looked like.

"Boy, open yo eyes!" Monique chided.

I still was not ready to see myself; yet, slowly, one by one, I opened my eyes. As my eyes began to allow in the bright light, I focused my eyes on my head. In the reflection of myself, I saw mounds of black hair resting on my head.

"What you think?!" Monique asked, eagerly.

I paused for a long moment without speaking.

"I put my foot in that shit, didn't I?" Monique said, complimenting herself.

I smiled in delight; more from seeing that I still had hair on my head than from the creativity of Monique's work.

I was not sure what to say. Although my hair had been relaxed, dyed a rich blue-black color, and styled to perfection, I looked strange to myself. As a teenager and young adult, I had worn effeminate hairstyles effortlessly. My young face had a freshness that complemented the hairdos well; however, as a twenty-eight year old man, I looked like a man who slipped on his wife's wig as a Halloween prank.

"…It looks nice," I managed to say.

"You don't like it?" Monique accurately surmised from the look on my face.

Hairstylists were artists, and, like any other artist, they were very sensitive about their work.

"No, it's not that I don't like it. I guess I just have to get used to seeing it," I said.

I had unintentionally bruised her ego.

"I had to cut off more of your hair than you wanted…" Monique said, searching for the reason as to my dislike.

"No, it's not the style at all," I said, comfortingly. "The hairstyle is beautiful. I probably need to shave this hair off of my face."

My statement was true: the hairstyle was beautiful, just not on me. It was also true that I needed to shave. Over the years of my confinement, I had begun to grow facial hair; a feat that I had never been able to accomplish when I was younger adult. Yet, it was not just the fact that I needed to shave that made my appearance look odd. While I still had a youthful appearance in many ways, my face had matured. My facial features had become slightly more masculine than the soft, boyish look of my youth.

"Okay, well, come in next week and I'll bump you out," Monique said, referring to washing and hot curling my hair.

"I will," I responded enthusiastically.

We hugged quickly before I rushed from the shop. My daddy had been waiting in his truck for me for over an hour. It was after ten o'clock p.m., when I left the beauty shop. I had spent nearly twelve hours getting my hair styled.

"Son, that's how you wanted your hair?" My daddy asked as I got in the truck.

I smiled, "Well, not really. I kind of wanted it like Anita Baker's hair of the eighties, but she had to cut off a lot of it."

"Oh," was my daddy's only response.

He did not like the hairstyle, though to prevent from hurting my feelings, he said nothing.

"Everybody's been asking about you. They're all over to your uncle's waiting for you."

Prior to being released from prison, I had asked my family to give me a coming-home party. After being released from prison, many inmates' families and friends would give them lavish parties to celebrate their re-entry into society. Tyler, my best friend with whom I was incarcerated, had sent me pictures of his coming-home party. The party was everything that we had dreamed it would be during our incarceration; every soul food dish one could name: from pies and cakes to fried chicken and macaroni and cheese. Though, most importantly, a huge host of his family members and friends had come to celebrate his release from confinement.

I could only imagine what my party would be like. I generally did not like to be the center of attention; however, I needed to feel special, if only for just one day. There were many times during my incarceration that I had felt unloved and unneeded; times in which I had gone several years without a single visitor; times that I did not know whether I would survive another day in captivity.

Prison life was uncertain. At any moment during the seven and a half years, I could have been raped, killed, or rendered insane. Yet, I had come through the horrific experience seemingly unscathed.

My uncle's condominium was picturesque. The building itself was a huge, wooden structure that accommodated dozens of families. It was located in the Old West End section of Toledo; an area where some of the oldest and largest Victorian-styled mansions were built.

I descended from my daddy's truck with trepidation. I did not know what to expect. A large part of me felt that there would be no celebration in my honor at all. Mymomme had already shared with me that I would be celebrating part of my homecoming party with my aunt who was celebrating her birthday on the same day as my release from prison. I was initially taken aback by the news. I secretly wanted to be celebrated alone. Though, as usual, I placed my feelings aside to be diplomatic.

In addition to Mymomme's revelation that my party would be shared, much more of my reservation had to do with my family's regard concerning my homecoming. While most of my family members had openly expressed their joy in having me home, those of whom I was closest had not seemed ecstatic in the manner that I had expected.

I wondered if they felt that I had placed myself in prison, because of the thoughtlessness of my action, and, as such, there was no need of a celebration for something that should not have ever occurred in the first place.

"*Ugh, let it go,*" I chided myself.

The truth of the matter was that my being incarcerated was of my own making. However, for me, the celebration did not lie in my returning home so much as it did that I had survived a horrendous ordeal. There were many, many times when I did not know whether

I would survive. I had known guys who were beaten with mop buckets until their skulls were split open. I knew of a correctional counselor who was gang-raped, beaten, and tortured for hours until she succumbed to death. I knew guys who were seemingly fine one moment and talking aloud to the voices in their minds the next moment. Yet, I had survived it all—and, for that, I felt, a celebration was in order.

The street was lined with cars. I shivered as I maneuvered my way through the cars in the parking lot and to the door of my uncle's home. I placed my hand on the doorknob, slowly turning it. I softly pushed open the door.

I stood back as I waited for a roar of voices to shout loudly, "Welcome home!"

Though, as the door opened creakingly, there was none.

Looking through the doorwell of the crowded condominium, it was clear to me that the party was in honor of my aunt's birthday and that my homecoming was merely an addition to her celebration.

I stepped into the crowded room unceremoniously and unnoticed. In a rush, all of the hurtful feelings that I had felt during my incarceration came to my mind, threatening to overwhelm me. I recalled the loneliness and the feelings of abandonment that I had felt while incarcerated. I had hoped that the feelings were a trick of the devil; that I was in fact loved and needed; that the days, weeks, months, and years that I had gone without letters or visits from my family were just figments of my imagination. However, as I entered my uncle's home, I knew that, in part, the feelings were valid. I was hurt. I blinked several times to force into submission the mist that had begun to cover my eyes. For the second time that day, I breathed in deeply, exhaled my sorrow, tucked away the pain I felt, and smiled broadly, as I began to mingle through the crowd of attendees.

Chapter Two

Life is seldom all that we want it to be. Oftentimes we have to mold our lives to fit our expectations. Marriages sometimes fail to be the fairytales that we imagined them to be when we were children; coveted careers can have their share of shortcomings; dream homes entail unfathomable responsibilities.

My homecoming was not what I had envisioned it to be while I was incarcerated; however, rather than to have dwelled on the negative aspects of what I expected my release to be, I chose to focus on the blessing of being home. I was free. I no longer had to subject myself to being told when to eat, when to sleep, or when to shower. I was free to make my own choices; to determine the course that my life would take.

~~~

I had a lot to accomplish: I needed to make my first appearance with my parole officer; I needed to attain my driver's license, which meant that I needed to take the written and maneuverability exam, again; and, I needed to purchase clothes to wear, since I had none.

I met with David Richmond, my parole officer, early on Monday morning. As an ex-offender, I was mandated to thirteen months of parole. The conditions of my parole were determined by my parole officer. For example, if I were a substance abuser, he could stipulate in my parole agreement that I attend weekly substance abuse meetings; or, if my case was related to domestic violence, he could have required that I seek mental health counseling related to domestic abuse. Because I had no issues, per se, no additional stipulations were attached to my parole, except to visit him weekly and to submit urine during each visit to maintain that I was not indulging in any illegal substances.

My appointment with Mr. Richmond was scheduled for eight o'clock a.m. My daddy and I arrived fifteen minutes early for the scheduled appointment. Twenty minutes after our arrival, the receptionist pushed a button to unlock the door which led to the parole officers' offices. Mr. Richmond greeted us as soon as we crossed the threshold of the door.

"How are you, Christopher? I'm David Richmond," he said, as he extended his hand for me to shake.

"Hi, Mr. Richmond. I am well." Turning in the direction of my daddy, "This is my father, Andrew."

"How's it going, sir?" Mr. Richmond asked, as he and my daddy shook hands.

"Not bad for an old guy," my daddy said, jokingly.

Mr. Richmond laughed at my daddy's remark, "You old? If you weren't standing next to this gentleman, I'd swear you were thirty years old."

My daddy and Mr. Richmond laughed good-naturedly as Mr.

Richmond escorted us to his office.

Mr. Richmond was a big man. He was at least 6'2 tall and about 250 lbs; yet, despite his size, he appeared to be as gentle as a lamb.

While my daddy and I were waiting in the outer office to be seen by Mr. Richmond, several of the guys in the waiting room had shared with me that Mr. Richmond was one of the meaner and stricter parole officers.

"Aww, man! You got that dude?!" One of the ex-offenders asked rhetorically. "Man, you ought to see if you can change parole officers! That dude ain't no joke!"

"Yeah, man," another guy chimed. "His ass come out to yo' house checking on you and shit, making sho' you staying where you say you stay and shit!"

"Shiiit, my dude had him and he p-v'd him, just because he missed one meeting!" A third guy said, indicating that someone had received a parole violation and was sent back to prison.

Strangely, Mr. Richmond did not appear to be anything like what the guys had described him as being. Despite his imposing size, he seemed very affable. He actually resembled a younger version of Saint Nick, with his rose-colored cheeks and hearty disposition. Perhaps, the other guys had pushed him too far and he had to resort to the tactics that he employed.

"Mr. Richmond…" My daddy began to say.

"Please, call me David," Mr. Richmond said, looking at my daddy and me.

"David," my daddy smiled. "As you are aware, my son and I have plans to have Chris' parole transferred to Atlanta where I live. In the meantime, we were wondering if he could be granted an out-of-state pass for one week so that he can visit with his sisters and step-mother at my home."

In order for a parolee to enter another state, he first had to receive permission from his parole officer. Failure to receive such permission was grounds for a parole violation in which the parolee could have been sent back to prison.

After serving six years of my sentence of nine to twenty-five years, my case was reviewed by the parole board. The parole board granted me a projected release date, which is similar to a parole, except, with paroles, inmates are released from prison two months after their parole hearing. Projected release dates can range from three months to three years or longer.

I was given a projected release date of eighteen months, which meant that I would be released after serving seven and a half years. My daddy and I had always planned that I would be released to his care, however, after we considered how long it would take to have my parole transferred to Georgia, my daddy asked Mother if I could be paroled to her home until my paperwork was complete.

While I was incarcerated, an addition had been added to our family. My stepmother, Sara, had given birth to my baby sister, Tatiyana. I now had two sisters. My first sister, Tiana, was born when I was sixteen.

As with my brothers, I had only seen them one time during my incarceration. I was anxious to see them.

"Sure, Mr. Price. How about I make the pass for two weeks? That way he can get reacquainted with his sisters," David offered.

"That'd be great, sir. I thank you for your hospitality," my daddy said, smiling.

"Well, if that's all, I will see you, sir, in two weeks. Enjoy your visit," David replied, amicably.

"Thank you, Mr....uh, David," I smiled.

"You're very welcome, Christopher."

~~~

I had made a vow to myself while I was incarcerated that I would visit with Mymomme as often as I could. I was torn about leaving for Atlanta so soon. A huge part of me wanted to begin rebuilding my life, but another part of me needed to be home where my family needed me.

I had nearly collapsed from heartache after seeing Mymomme at my homecoming party. She was grotesquely thin. Mymomme had always enjoyed a beautiful, curvaceous body. While remnants of her curves were still evident beneath her short skirt, she was far smaller than her usual weight. In addition to her drastic weight loss, her hair was incredibly thin and her skin was ashen, as if all of the moisture had been drained from her once radiant, dark brown skin.

"Welcome home, baby," Mymomme greeted me in a heavy, gravelly voice with her arms outstretched.

As I firmly embraced Mymomme, it seemed as though I could feel every one of the bones of her back. After we disengaged, I stood back watching her as she danced in excitement of my return home. Her movements were erratic; jittery. I watched her, analyzing her behavior. The pieces of the puzzle falling into place: she was under the influence of drugs.

For as long as I could remember, Mymomme had abused drugs: alcohol, marijuana, crack-cocaine, cocaine, or pills. Her issue with drugs was not news to me. Yet, I had never known for drugs to have the effect on her that they did. When I was a child, she was not the most responsible adult or parent; yet, despite her addiction to drugs, she had managed to attain employment and to pay her bills.

Times had changed. The clearest indication for me that she had lost the battle to substance abuse was found in her appearance. Mymomme had always shown special attention to the way she looked. Her smooth, mahogany-colored skin and big, flawless smile were her pride. She had the body of an African queen. She would walk into any room as though she owned it. During the 70s, whenever the Commodores' hit song *Brick House* would air on the radio, Mymomme would stop mid-action and parade around the room as though the song was written specifically for her! The song described a well-endowed and perfectly proportionate woman's figure of 36-24-36.

However, Mymomme's physical qualities were a glimmer of the past: her body no longer turned heads; her smile no longer brightened rooms. Her entire being seemed to be crying out for help. She did not look like she could physically survive much longer in such condition.

~~~

I walked from Mother's house to Mymomme's house. The walk was not long, and I needed it. I loved walking. It gave me time to think. As I walked down the familiar streets, I continued to marvel at how the homes had aged and the streets had become more worn since before I was incarcerated.

Arriving at Mymomme's house, I walked up the stairs to the porch. Again, I thought, the house had not changed much at all. It looked abandoned. It was hard to believe that it was inhabited at all, let alone by my mother.

The peach-colored paint had fallen from the house in chips. I reached for the doorknob of the aluminum screen door, yet there was none. Instead, a shoestring was used in place of the doorknob. Pulling the shoestring, the screen door swung open aimlessly without much effort from me at all. I knocked on the old, wooden door, waiting for someone to answer.

As I waited, I continued to survey the house. The front windows of the house were cracked in several places. I walked precariously across the loose floorboards of the porch to the other end. I tried to peak around the house, however the shaky banister prevented me from doing so. Just as I began to walk back to the front door, it groaned open.

"Aww, hey, bae," Mymomme greeted. "I thought I heard somebody knocking," she said, stepping aside so that I could enter the house.

Unsurprisingly, the interior of the house was nice and cozy. She had bought new furniture since I had been gone. The crème and peach floral print of the sofa blended with the soft-colored walls beautifully. As I crossed the living room to the dining room, the floors squeaked beneath the carpet. Looking to my right, I smiled inwardly when I saw the big, black radiator in the corner of the small dining room. Despite being an eyesore, I had to admit that it was incredibly efficient; the entire house was toasty warm. I sat down at the dining room table.

"Be careful! Those chairs loose! I keep telling Sam to tighten 'em, but he still ain't did it."

Just as she had spoken Sam's name, he emerged from the bedroom.

"Hey there. I didn't know you were here," I greeted.

"What's going on, my brother?" He smiled, revealing a gold tooth.

"Not too much," I responded.

Sam was Mymomme's boyfriend. They had been in a relationship for nearly fifteen years. I watched him as he crossed the room to give me a hug. His tall, thin frame glided across the room like a slender gazelle.

"How you been?" He asked.

I stood up from my seat to embrace him.

"I been good. Trying to get used to being home," I said as I smiled.

I liked Sam. With the exception of one time that I was aware, he had never mistreated Mymomme. He seemed to understand her in a way that her previous partners had not understood her. Although he shared in Mymomme's abuse of drugs, I did not blame him. While I knew that he was not an entirely positive influence in her life, I recognized that she would use drugs whether she was with him or not, and that she was chemically dependent long before he had come into her life.

"You seen your brother?" He asked, referring to Miah-Miah.

"No. I was just about to ask Mymomme where he was."

"Shoot, I don't know. You know that boy stay in the streets. They probably gone be locking him up before long," she expressed, lowering her head. "Just as soon as one of my kids come home, the other one go away."

Her slight, malnourished body began to heave as she sobbed. I felt sorry for her. Life had not been kind to her.

Miah-Miah was ten years old when I was jailed. During the years of my confinement, he had been in juvenile jail many times for various criminal acts: drug distribution, fighting, truancy. He had no relationship with his biological father and his mother was addicted to drugs. His young life was filled with hurt.

Prior to being incarcerated, I was not just Miah-Miah's brother. In many ways, I was a father-figure to him. I reprimanded him when he had misbehaved, encouraged him when he struggled with life, and applauded him when he did well. Because of my incarceration, he lost his only true source of stability.

"It's going to be okay, Mymomme. I'll see what I can learn about his case and what kind of representation he's receiving."

"Okay, bae," she replied in a low, grief-filled voice.

I stayed at Mymomme's a few minutes longer. I informed her that I was leaving with my daddy for a couple of weeks. As expected, she did not take the news well. She needed and wanted me home in Toledo. I was conflicted between the needs of my family and a strong desire to help myself and, thereby, them. I chose the greater good.

Chapter Three

The strong scent of pine filled my nostrils, rousing me from my slumber. I awakened to be greeted by huge, thirty-feet, tall trees. I opened the sunroof of my daddy's truck so that I could look at the Georgian sky. It was beautiful: silver stars sprinkled across a black backdrop. I felt alive, exuberant, as I breathed in the sweet aroma. As though, for the first time since being released from prison, I was at home. I connected with the southern state in a way that startled me. I felt like I belonged there; it was if I had been there before in a different time.

Looking across the vast land of trees and mountains, I imagined a time when my foreparents were forcibly confined to the region. In my mind's eye, I saw them as they toiled the land under the hot, blazing sun. I cringed at the sight of their flesh being ripped from their backs with leather whips bound by evil hands. I watched as my uncles and aunts' innards were violated by a people who saw them as no more than harnessed mules. I felt as though the blood-soaked Earth of my ancestors cried out to me, "You are home, my child!"

Yet, despite the horrors of my people's experience, I had a strong sensation that my beginnings would come forth on the land.

Two hours after crossing the Tennessean state line into Georgia, the landscape gave way to Atlanta's beautiful skyline. At only five in the morning, the city had already begun to bustle with energy.

Vehicles lined the entrance ramps, awaiting their opportunity to merge onto the already congested highway.

Atlanta was so very different from Toledo. It reminded me in many ways of what Washington, D.C. meant to me when I lived there for a brief time as a teenager with Sara and my father. Blacks of all socioeconomic statuses occupied the areas: from the very wealthy to the severely impoverished. The cities showcased the best of talent in Black America. African American politicians, entertainers, doctors, lawyers, educators, and businesspersons graced the land in their varied regalia. They were sights to see; towns worth experiencing.

~~~

Thirty minutes after exiting Atlanta's city limits, my daddy and I arrived in the suburban city of his home. My daddy's home was very nice. Like his truck, the house looked exactly as it had in the photos that he had sent to me during my imprisonment. The lot on which his home sat was huge in comparison to those in Toledo.

Stepping down from the truck, I stretched for a long moment. My legs and back were tight with tension. After I had successfully relieved my muscles of their agony, I breathed in the Georgian air, again. The air smelled and felt differently than did the air in Ohio. It was, of course, much warmer and more humid in Georgia than Ohio. The scent of the huge trees, for which the state was known, added to the state's allurement, making it more welcoming.

I walked to a fence that surrounded the backyard. The space was expansive. Although, it did not contain a pool, it was large enough to accommodate one and still have plenty of room to entertain during the autumn months.

"Son, you ready to help me to take the luggage into the house," my daddy asked, interrupting my thoughts.

"Yes," I replied.

As I entered the kitchen from the garage, I was immediately engulfed with a familiar scent. I smiled. Like Mother's home, my daddy's house smelled of mothballs. The fragrance was not overwhelming, though it was definitely noticeable.

"You can put your things downstairs in the basement. There is a bedroom to the left of the staircase and a living area to the right," he instructed.

"Okay, thanks.

I slowly walked down the squeaky stairs to the basement. I looked to my left to see an entryway into a room. Stepping into the room and turning on the light, I saw an adequate-sized room with a large bed positioned in the middle of the room and nightstands on each side of the bed. A huge dresser was placed on the adjacent wall, which served no purpose for me at the time, since I had no real possessions, save a couple of jogging suits that my daddy had purchased for me.

In the living quarters, there was a big television, two sofas, and an office area with two desks and a desktop computer.

Since my sisters and step-mother were still asleep, I decided to go back to sleep and to greet them once they returned home from school. I was anxious to know what our first meeting would be like: who were they were as individuals; how had life in the suburbs under my daddy and Sara's parenting shaped them; what did they know of their older brother who was incarcerated? I had many questions for them, yet I contained my curiosity, forcing myself to sleep.

~~~

I was disoriented. I looked around myself in vain. The windowless room was completely dark, making it more difficult for me to ascertain where I was. I sat completely still for a moment until my thoughts became clearer. I remembered. I was in my daddy's home in Georgia.

The past couple of weeks were filled with a whirlwind of activity. I had gone from absolute confinement to being free. The realization of being home still baffled me. I had always hoped and prayed that the day would come in which I would be released, yet it still seemed surreal. I felt like I was in a dream.

Arching my back as I stretched, I pulled the covers back and positioned myself to stand. I felt blessed: Mother had gladly received me into her home; I awakened each morning on a soft bed and in a peaceful state-of-mind; I did not have to worry about whether I would be jarred from sleep by COs who sought to make the lives of inmates worse than what they already were.

My daddy had provided me with all of my essential necessities: toiletries, socks, underwear, a coat, hat, and sweat suits to wear until I was able to expand my wardrobe. I had left the walls of Lima Correctional Institution with nothing, save a paper bag filled with memorabilia that I had kept over the years. Sitting on the bed, deep in thought, I was made aware of the fact that I had all I needed: food, clothing, shelter, and the love of my family.

I rose from the bed and ascended the stairs to the main level, I looked around the house. The house was not a mansion, by any stretch of the imagination, but, in comparison to the 6x9 cell that had been my home for the past seven years, it was humongous. The laundry room, a large eat-in kitchen, a living room with a fireplace, a formal dining room, and a powder room were on the main level, while three bedrooms a full bath and master en suite were on the upper level.

I was pleased for my daddy and Sara. They had successfully created a comfortable lifestyle for themselves.

As I descended the stairs of the upper level, I heard the door open in the kitchen.

"Hey, son. Are you just waking up?" My daddy asked, leaving the door agape as he entered.

"Yes. I was tired for some reason," I responded.

"Well, the trip down here will do that to you. Ten hours on the road can be taxing," he stated.

I heard the sound of shuffling feet and rustling bags coming from inside the garage, followed by car doors closing. Seconds later, a small bundle of energy and personality walked into the room.

"Hi, Chris!" A little girl exclaimed through a missing front tooth.

"Hey there, Tatiyana!" I smiled broadly, extending my hand for her to shake.

She placed her small hand around my fingers, shaking them, enthusiastically.

"You know who I am?" I asked in delight.

Placing her small hand on her imaginary hip, she responded smartly, "Of course, you're my big brother!"

Her simple words warmed my heart.

"Are you going to live with us? Daddy said you're going to live with us."

"I don't know. It depends on how nicely you treat me," I said in jest.

She folded her arms and looked at me through narrowed eyelids, "Humph!"

I laughed. She was adorable.

I was taken aback by her level of comfort with me. She regarded me as though I had always been a part of her existence. When my daddy and Sara had brought my sisters and Corey to see me, she was only a few months shy of a year old; yet, apparently, my daddy and Sara had kept the memory of me alive more than I was aware.

Just then, Sara and Tiana walked into the house. I stood to hug them.

"Hi, Sara," I said as I hugged her firmly.

"Hi, Chris," Sara smiled. "How have you been?" She asked.

I smiled. "I've been good…better now that I'm home," I laughed.

"Hi, Tiana!" I beamed.

"Hi, Chris," Tiana responded, shyly.

"I don't know why she acting shy. You should have seen her when they said you were going to prison!" My daddy exclaimed.

"Huh?" I responded, confusingly.

"Remember when you were given your conviction?" My daddy asked.

"Yes…"

"The television stations aired the trial on the News. After the conviction was read by the judge, Tiana broke down crying."

"Did she?" I asked, sadly.

"Yeah, I did. I remember that day! I know I was too young to really know what all was going on, but I remember feeling really sad," Tiana confided in a soft voice.

I simultaneously felt an overpowering sense of joy and sadness. I was happy that she cared enough about me to be moved to tears because of my situation, yet another part of me was hurt that I had caused my sister so much pain.

She was only six years old when I was sentenced; though, I guess, she was old enough to know that her brother was being taken away from her. I walked over to where she stood and gave her a big hug.

"Thank you for loving me."

"You're welcome," Tiana smiled as we embraced.

"So what's going on with your hair?" She asked as we separated.

I laughed. One moment we were having a heart-warming

conversation, the next we were talking about my hideous hair.

"Well, I was going to try modeling. People say that it's difficult for ex-offenders to get work out here, so I figured I'd go back to what I know and, since I had modeled a little before I went to prison, I thought I'd pick it up again. I wanted something edgy that would set me apart from the other male models."

"Oh, I see!" She said, excitedly.

"But, I'm about to cut this stuff off!"

"Oh, why!" She said, disappointedly.

"Because this crap is a mess! I don't know how to style it between beautician visits; I sleep wildly, so the scarf always comes off my head at night; when I take a shower, my ends get wet and nappy; plus, it's expensive having permed hair and going to the beauty shop and stuff. I need a job just to maintain my hair!"

"Oh, I thought it was good idea for the modeling."

"Yeah, it was, but now is not a good time for me to do the style. I need an income."

"Oh, okay," she said, thoughtfully.

~~~

True to my word, I cut my hair the following day after my conversation with Tiana. I could not take having hair any longer. I was used to having a short, nicely tapered faded-cut. Too much maintenance is involved in having long hair. I liked to brush my hair and to keep moving.

I had true African hair: the kind that could look at the hot autumn sun and dare it to say something! My hair was not just nappy, but it was also dry—desert dry. So, I had to drench it with water before I could even think about applying any kind of grease, otherwise the moisturizer would just sit on top of my hair in white patches, like Danny Glover's hair in the movie *The Color Purple*!

Quite naturally, when my daddy offered for me to allow Leslie, his barber and good friend, to cut my hair, I said, "Yes!"

"How you want it, Chris?" Leslie asked the following evening.

Ordinarily, I was very particular about who cut my hair, but I trusted Leslie. He was not only my daddy's friend, but he was also the father of my cousin's child. Plus, anything had to look better than what it looked like at the time, I rationalized.

"Cut it all off, but long enough so that I can get waves," I said proudly as I sat on a chair in my daddy's basement. I was as happy as a child in a candy store! I could not wait! I had gone way too long with hair on my head.

An half of an hour later, "Take a look at it. Tell me what you think," Leslie stated.

Barbers always amused me when they instructed us to look at our hair after it was cut, particularly when we received short cuts like mine. There was very little that we patrons could say or do: all of our hair was gone. It was not as though we could make our hair magically reappear and ask them to re-cut it in the event that they had made a mistake. So, unless they had done something really crazy, I usually looked at my hair in the mirror just to appease them.

"It looks good. Thanks!" I said, smiling.

I did not want it quite as short as it was. It was my hope that my brush-waves would still be visible, but what could I do, make my hair magically reappear??

"It'll look better in a couple days. I had to cut the perm out," Leslie expressed, as though reading my mind.

"Okay. It's cool. I'll just re-train it, so that the waves are back in there. I appreciate you."

~~~

I felt great. It was a welcome relief having my hair cut. I decided to continue with my plan to pursue modeling, despite having short hair. I needed to have photos taken, so that I could create a portfolio to present to modeling agencies.

I had no idea how to choose a good photographer, so I called one of my best friends, Leonard. As a beautician and a performer, he was active in the entertainment industry and was bound to know a photographer.

"Leeza?" I said into the phone receiver.

"Hey, chile. What you doin?"

"Nothing. Down here in Atlanta still. I need a photographer."

"A photographer? What you need a photographer for?"

"I told you that I was going to try modeling."

"Oh. Yea. What yo' head looking like?" He asked in his

Floridian accent.

I laughed. "I cut off my hair."

"Chile, I'm so glad you did! That shit was a mess! I don't know why Monique did that shit to yo' head! I called up to dat damn shop and told Monique she shouldna done that shit!" Leonard fumed.

"She didn't know. She just did what I asked," I laughed.

"Her ass knew better! That shit played out! You runnin' around here looking like a damn pimp! She know dey don't wear no shit like dat no mo'! Her ass was being funny!"

I could not stop laughing! He was livid!

"No, she wasn't. I told her to do it like that," I said through tears of laughter.

"Chile, well, she shoulda told yo ass hell naw!" He replied, passionately.

"I thought it looked nice," I said, humorously.

"Yea, the style was cute, but not on you! You needed something more masculine. I said, 'they don't do that shit no mo'! Anyway, chile, what you call me fo'?!"

I was laughing so hard that I could hardly breathe. His entire family acted just like him: his sister, brother, and his mother. They were tough as nails, but as sweet as honey. They would help anyone in need or want. Ms. Maple, his mother, was always allowing someone to live with them. The boarder had either lost his job, was evicted, or his boyfriend beat him and put him out of their home. For whatever reasons, people always found a way to find themselves at Ms. Maple's doorstep.

Prior to my incarceration, I, too, had lived with her. I had family with whom I could have lived, but Ms. Maple's home was always so welcoming. I loved them as though they were my own family.

"A photographer. I need a photographer."

"Oh, chile, dats right…call dis number and ask for Lamont. He live in Atlanta. Tell him you know me and for him to give you a good deal."

"Who is he? Y'all wasn't messin' around was y'all?" I asked, insinuating that he and the guy were involved sexually.

"Chile, hell naw! I don't fuck wit no damn queens!" Leonard shouted in near disgust at my mock suggestion of him being intimate with an effeminate gay guy.

A clicking sound was heard through the phone receiver.

"Hello…hello…hello??"

And, just like that he had disconnected the phone call. No goodbye or anything, just click and he was gone. I laughed until tears nearly flowed from my eyes. He was funny.

~~~

Two days later, my daddy and I had arrived at Lamont's studio. Like most photo shoots, the session was grueling. Professional models make photo-taking look easy. When, in truth, they are not. An average session lasts about three to four hours. The hours may seem miniscule, though the process is very tedious. Smiling and striking poses for several hours can get tiresome very quickly.

The upside was that Lamont was an excellent photographer. He was very professional and he knew his craft well. After the shoot, I was able to look at the photos through the lens of his digital camera. It was interesting looking at myself in the photos. Although they were shot well, I did not look like myself to me. Strangely, I had expected to see the image of the person I was eight years ago. Instead, I saw someone who was older and more mature. Photography is fascinating in that regard. While I had seen myself many times in the mirrors in prison and since I had been home, mirrors were not quite able to capture the image of the person I had become as did the photos.

~~~

"Hi, Sara," I said, greeting my step-mother as I entered the kitchen from the garage.

"Hey, Chris. How are you?" Sara asked.

"I'm fine; just I'm a little tired. That photo shoot was exhausting. Whose car is that outside?"

Sara smiled at me innocently, "You've got company downstairs."

"Huh? Who is it?" I asked, curiously.

I could not imagine who was there to visit me. I did not know anyone who lived in Atlanta, other than my friend, Erin, and he had not mentioned anything about visiting me.

"I don't know," she smiled. You'll have to go downstairs to see."

I walked down the stairs of the basement. Instinctively, as I stepped down from the last stair, I looked to the left of the staircase, in the direction of the bedroom. A voluptuous woman sat on the bed with her legs crossed seductively. I blinked several times to be certain that the person I saw was real.

"Hi, Chris," she said, smiling sweetly.

I smiled back uncertainly; unsure that my eyes were not deceiving me.

"Hi," I responded, cautiously.

"How you been?!" She said as she leapt from the bed with arms spread a part for me to embrace her.

I received her into my arms. She squeezed me tightly for a long moment and then without warning, she kissed me fervently. I pulled away from her slightly.

"I've been good," I said, as I positioned myself to look at her. I felt uncomfortable.

She grabbed my hand, ushering me to the bed. I followed obligingly.

"You look so good! I love your goatee!" She said, touching my face.

"Thank you," I smiled, shyly. "Karen, how did you know I was here?" I asked.

Karen was my ex-girlfriend. She and I met when we were in

college. I ended our relationship while I was in the county jail. I had tried to maintain the relationship, but fighting for my life and maintaining a romantic relationship proved to be too much for me. Karen and I had kept in touch with one another over the years of my confinement, though not consistently.

"I called Ms. Randle and she told me," she said.

"Oh."

I did not know what to say. I was pleased to see Karen, albeit surprised. We had not spoken or written to each other in a couple of years. Her visit came as a shock to me. I would have expected to have chatted with her first to catch up on our lives before seeing her.

"So how have you been?!" Karen asked excitedly as she reached for my other hand.

"I've been good; just trying to get re-acclimated to being home."

"You haven't been institutionalized, have you?" She asked, softly.

I laughed, "No!"

"Oh, I was just asking, because I saw on this movie how this guy killed himself, because he couldn't cope with being home from prison."

Many people compared prison life in movies with reality. Although there was some validity to what Hollywood portrayed in film, the films still fell short of reality.

I laughed, again. "No, I'm not going to commit suicide. I wouldn't allow myself to become so engrossed in my surroundings in prison that I would become institutionalized. Besides, I had waited far too long for the day to come when I'd be released to extinguish the joy of freedom by killing myself."

"Oh, okay, I just wanted to know," Karen stated, solemnly.

I laughed to myself. Her question regarding being institutionalized had obviously been weighing heavily on her mind. It was obviously a legitimate concern of hers. I had been incarcerated for seven and a half years—more than enough time for someone to become overly-engrossed in his environment.

"I have something else I want to ask you," she said, excitedly.

"Okay," I replied, waiting as she rummaged through her purse.

A part of me should have known what was coming next; however, nothing in my wildest of dreams could have prepared me for the moment. I had seen the scene depicted in movies many times, but never in reality.

"Will you marry me?" Karen asked softly with a huge smile on her face.

"Huh?" I laughed unintentionally, a bit from nervousness, though more from the absurdity of her request. "Uh, Karen, we don't know each other anymore…I've been gone for seven years…uhm…I've grown and changed in ways that even I am unaware…you don't know what I've done in there…if I have any diseases…you need to get to know me, and I need to get to know you."

Karen's feelings were hurt. Although I meant all that I said, I had expressed myself a little too passionately. It was not my intention to wound her, yet I could not fathom what would compel her to ask me to marry her. Our meeting was the first that we had seen of each other since I was in the county jail over seven years ago.

While we had written one another over the years, the letters were sporadic, and they oftentimes were fueled by the pain she felt from the break-ups with any one of her beaus at the time. She had also conceived and birthed a child during my incarceration. While I had no problem with being a father to a child that was not biologically my own, as her husband, she should have first considered what kind of father I would be to her daughter before she even entertained the thought of marriage.

"Karen, I'm sorry. I didn't mean to hurt you, but you don't ask someone to marry you after you've gone seven years without seeing him. I understand that you may have been influenced by the love that we shared, but you need to know the man that I am today. You didn't ask me any of the questions that every woman should ask a man who's been incarcerated: Did I have sex with other men while confined? Was I in a relationship with anyone in there? Do I have any sexually transmitted diseases?"

"Well, do you?" She asked, pointedly.

I chuckled aloud; more so, from disbelief that I had to mention what she should have known to ask of me than from amusement with her question. "No, I don't have any STD's...Yes, I was in relationships in there and, yes, I did have sex while I was in there, but those are things that you should have asked me. My point in stating the questions is that I shouldn't have had to instruct you on what you should want and need to know about me."

"Oh, okay." Karen replied.

She was satisfied. The person that physically sat across from her and the person that she remembered him to be was enough for her. It seemed that the candor with which I spoke had confirmed what she felt in her heart and soul: I was the man for her.

Chapter Four

Returning home from prison was much like being an adolescent, again. Life seemed brand new. The excitement of accomplishing previously achieved feats was thrilling to me. Things that most adults regarded as mundane were major markers in my transition from being bound to free.

My daddy and I arrived back in Toledo exactly two weeks after we had left for Atlanta. I came home just in time to take my driver's test. After having successfully passed the written portion of the driver's test, I was left to complete the maneuverability portion. I was far more nervous about passing the test this time around than I was when I was younger.

I arrived at the testing center minutes before my scheduled exam. The driving instructor called my name from the front door of the license bureau. Her demeanor was cold. She was a middle-aged White woman, with fading brown hair that was snatched tightly into a bun on the back of her head.

"Christopher Price!" She commanded.

"Yes, that's me," I said, as I approached her.

"Follow me," she bellowed.

I walked closely behind her as she exited through the glass doors of the facility and to the parking lot.

"Where is the vehicle you will be driving?" She asked.

"It's right over here," I replied.

I escorted her toward my daddy's truck, an extremely unlikely vehicle in which to take a maneuverability exam, though it was the only vehicle available to me at the time. As we neared the truck, the instructor had a look of astonishment on her face. I watched her as she took in the enormity of the truck.

Shaking her head in disbelief, she told me to get into the truck and to turn on the signal lights. I did as I was told. She walked around the vehicle, writing on a tablet as she inspected the truck. After she was finished, she climbed into the truck. Although I had already adjusted my mirrors, I did so again. I fastened my seatbelt and waited for her instructions.

"You may turn on the vehicle," she instructed, kindly.

I did not know what catastrophic event had occurred in the hemisphere, but she had changed. Her countenance was softer; her voice had a tone of cordiality. I surmised that perhaps she pitied me for having to take the test in a spaceship.

"Please, exit the parking lot."

I cautiously placed the gear in the drive position and inched out of the parking space. I slowly drove to the street. I stopped at the entrance to the boulevard, awaiting further directions.

"Make a left. Be sure to watch for oncoming traffic," she cautioned, nervously.

I laughed to myself. Traffic was bustling. The blank slate on the instructor's face was replaced with dread. Until then, I did know that she was capable of emitting such an emotion.

I waited for a long moment before I entered the street. Traffic was horrendous. I did not want to take any chances of failing. After an eternity had seemingly passed, I merged into traffic. The instructor exhaled sharply, visibly relaxing.

"Make a right at the traffic light."

I made a series of right and left turns until we were back in the parking lot of the license bureau. I was instructed to drive to the rear of the building where the cones were placed for parallel parking.

I drove the truck to the designated spot. I waited for her instructions.

"You must parallel park the vehicle."

The instructor was not allowed to give any instructions as to how I was to achieve the feat. Yet, after reading a diagram in the building, I understood that I had to drive between four cones, stop, place the vehicle in reverse, circle the cones, stop in front of a single cone at the top of the pyramid, and then back into an allotted space between the four cones; all in one fluid motion!

"Okay," I said.

Oh, God, I thought! I breathed in and out deeply. The moment of truth had arrived. Driving the truck on the streets was easy, however maneuvering between the cones would be challenging.

I took one more deep breath in and slowly exhaled. I placed the gear of the truck in drive. I completed the first of her instructions rather effortlessly; however, I was incredibly anxious about having to parallel park. I could not hit any of the cones. Hitting even one of the cones meant that I had failed the test.

I slowly swerved around the single cone, taking great care not to hit it. I looked through my side mirrors, gauging how much clearance I had between the cones. I had very little space. The truck was too big for me. The steering was too gentle; an advantage of driving a newer truck, but a disadvantage in that it took very little effort to turn the wheel. Applying too much force to the steering wheel and I would shoot pass the cone, missing my only opportunity to get between the cones safely without hitting any of them.

Ever so gently, I eased my foot off the brake pedal and turned the steering wheel. I moved the truck at a snail's pace. Before I knew it, I was between the cones! I placed the truck in reverse, moving from between the cones. I did it! My instinct was to jump from the truck and shout, hallelujah! Yet, I remained composed until the instructor had exited the truck and had given me a slip of paper that detailed any mistakes I may have made.

I looked down at the piece of paper. She deducted two points from my overall score: one point for having taken too long to enter traffic; and, one for entering traffic in the outside lane.

"Congratulations, Mr. Price, you passed the test."

For a split second, I was taken aback by the pointed deductions. If I had I entered traffic sooner than I did, she would have been screaming for Jesus! Yet, rather than to make a fuss about one single point, I gladly accepted the piece of paper from her hand! I had my driver's license! I felt like a child on Christmas!!!

"Prison friendships don't last outside the walls of the penitentiary, son." My daddy had stated, matter-of-factly. *"Y'all can be the best of friends in the joint, but, once y'all leave, y'all will go your separate ways."*

I listened to my daddy disbelievingly. I felt that my friendship with Tyler was unlike typical friendships; he and I were unlike typical inmates.

Yet, as I lay on my bed thinking about what my daddy had said to me years ago, I wondered if there had been some truth to what he expressed. I had been home for several days and I had yet to see Tyler.

In prison, Tyler and I had been like peanut butter and jelly; we were inseparable. We were like brothers. Together, we had weathered the storms of prison life: we encouraged one another when times were rough; we hoped and dreamed for a better future for each other; and, we had helped each other deal with the pain of our families' issues.

Although, I had not spoken to Tyler a great deal after his release from prison two years prior, I felt that there was a logical explanation for his near-desertion of me. Life as a free man had not been kind to him. It was, as he had explained, anything but what we had dreamt it to be. Employment was virtually impossible to attain, which meant that money was difficult to earn; responsibilities escalated; and, familial relationships had changed—in short, life had not been a cakewalk for him. Yet, in spite of his hardships, I had expected to see him upon my release from prison. However, weeks had gone by and I still had not seen him.

Then, as though the Holy Spirit granted the longings of my spirit, Tyler arrived unannounced at my Aunt Carol's home on a cool, sunny day.

"What's up?!" I said, before I had fully exited the house.

I was excited to see him. So much had transpired since the time of his release from prison. I was anxious to share with him all that had gone on in my life. I galloped down the few stairs of the porch to greet him.

"What's up?" I repeated as I shook his outstretched hand, hugging him with my free arm.

"Nothing much, man." Pointing behind himself, "This my girl, Ariel. Ariel this my dude, Chris. We was locked up together at Lima," he said, introducing Ariel and me.

"It's good to meet you, Ariel," I said, smiling, as we shook hands.

"What's been up? How you feel being a free man?" Tyler asked.

"It's been cool. I'm happy to be home, just trying to get used to it all," I said.

"Yeah, man, it take some getting used to. Shit ain't been easy out here. You got to make it the best way you can. Man, you shoulda caught me when Houston came out. I was balling then. Shit, my pockets on low now. I'm struggling trying to pay me and Ariel bills, plus, take care of these kids we got."

"It's cool. Don't worry about it. My daddy been looking out for me."

Something had changed. I could not quite express what I sensed, but something was different in Tyler; in our friendship. He seemed to be the same old Tyler in many ways. His laughter was still infectious; he still appeared to be kind-hearted; he was still forthright, yet something was amiss. Our conversations were not as free-flowing as they had once been. We conversed as though we were old acquaintances, rather than good friends. He seemed to look for things to say to me as opposed to the ease in dialogue in which we had once shared.

After several minutes of talking about our families, Tyler announced that he had an errand to fulfill.

"All right, man, I'ma get outta here. I got to make a run about some money."

"Okay. Thanks for stopping by. It was good to meet you, Ariel," I said as I alternated between hugging them.

As I watched Tyler and Ariel get in their car and begin to drive away, I thought of my former friendship with Tyler. Our friendship had sustained me during my most troublesome times in prison. Tyler was a gift from Heaven whose friendship had helped to positively guide my steps. I had always imagined that we would embark upon the voyage of life beyond the walls of prison together. However, despite my earnest of attempts, I felt in my spirit that I had lost something precious; something that I would not get back.

~~~

Christmas was by far my favorite holiday. It was the time of the year where most everyone was in a festive and giving mood.

Although the holiday had become heavily commercialized with stores capitalizing on the gift-giving spirit of the season, it still embodied the meaning of Christmas: the day that Christ had given Himself for humankind.

I had chosen to stay in Toledo to spend Christmas with my maternal family, the Randles. The holiday was everything that I had hoped it to be while I was confined. As was our tradition, we all met at Mama's house. Mama prepared a wonderful meal: chicken, dressing, candied yams, greens, ham, chitterlings, banana pudding, cakes and pies.

Although the food looked and smelled delicious, I did not eat half of what I wanted to eat. Meals in prison were not fried or heavily seasoned. As such, I became nauseous after eating certain foods, particularly fast food and soul food dishes which were laden in fat, butter, and sugar.

Aside from finicky stomach, I thoroughly enjoyed myself. One of the blessings of the holiday season is that it gave families a reason to congregate and to share in the joy of being around one another.

My cousins, Booger and Tookie, were amongst my other family members that were present at the Christmas dinner. I saw both of them regularly as they either worked or lived in the same vicinity where Mother lived. Booger attained a job at McDonald's. His achievement of an Associate's degree in business while he was incarcerated placed him the position to be a manager of the restaurant. I enjoyed walking to Booger's workplace and seeing him clad in his managerial uniform and instructing his employees.

The sight of Booger being responsible and making a productive life for himself allowed me to better accept his unfair incarceration. He and his childhood girlfriend, Niecy, had resumed their romantic relationship and were expecting their first child.

I felt a bit of comfort in knowing that Booger was doing well for himself in spite of his unjust bout with the criminal justice system. I had always felt that he should have never been jailed. Yet, despite me having testified during our trial that he was not the person who had shot and killed Adam Faulkner, the jury still found Booger guilty of involuntary manslaughter. I believed that a part of me would always feel responsible for the seven years of his life that were taken away from him.

Tookie amused me. She handled her release far differently than what I had expected of her. In fact, she behaved more in the manner that guys typically did when they were released. She partied a great deal and entertained the advances of men. She celebrated her release in a way that Booger and I did not. We were focused on making up for the time that we had lost while we were confined in a responsible manner. Tookie, however, chose to embrace her release from prison differently.

Mama had a particularly difficult time accepting Tookie's behavior.

"Baby, I just don't know about that girl," Mama confided to me.

"What do you mean?" I asked.

"That girl comes in here all times of the night, drinking and smoking or whatever she out there doing. She don't clean the kitchen or nothing!" She expressed.

"Oh…Well, maybe she's just enjoying her time being home," I suggested.

"She ain't got no time for that! She need to be gettin' her a job, so she can find a place of her own and gettin' Lolita back!" Mama said, referring to Tookie's daughter.

While Tookie was confined, she had naively given custody of Lolita to the child's paternal grandmother. After her release from prison, Lolita's grandmother refused to give her back to Tookie. As a result, a custody battle ensued between Tookie and Lolita's grandmother.

"She's trying to get Lita back, but you know custody battles are hard. And, she told me that she just got a job. I think she just needed time to party and stuff after being locked-up for so long," I offered.

"You and Booger didn't need no time to party and shit!" Mama laughed, despite herself. She did not intend to get so emotionally riled. "I just don't like it, Christopher. A young lady ain't supposed to be acting like that."

"Well, everybody's time in prison affects him or her differently. When I came home, I wanted to put my best foot forward to make up for all the time I had lost. I guess that was the case with Booger, too. Tookie just needed some time to be young and free. She'll be okay. You'll see," I replied, optimistically.

"Well, I sho hope so, baby," Mama conceded.

~~~

Mother had gone to North Carolina to spend Christmas with her oldest child, Aunt Harriet. She returned home to Toledo a very different woman than the one who had left just a week prior.

"Chris!" Mother yelled my name from the kitchen early one morning.

I hurriedly rose from bed and rushed downstairs.

"Yes, ma'am?" I said as I entered the kitchen.

"Make me something to eat. I'm hungry," she stated, flatly.

"Okay," I said, obligingly.

I looked around the kitchen. It looked as if a tornado had been unleashed. It was in complete disarray: unused pots and pans were on the kitchen table, food from the refrigerator and cupboards were on the countertops, a broom was laid on the floor beside a mound of sugar where Mother had apparently attempted to clean the mess, but was able to complete the job. The electric stove was turned on high. Four thick slices of bacon sizzled in a large skillet that partially covered one of the eyes of the stove.

I was bewildered. Mother was not only known for being extremely meticulous, but she was also fiercely independent. I had never known for her to ask someone to prepare a meal for her. I looked at her as she sat in a chair at the kitchen table trying to pour sugar into a coffee cup. Her hair, which had never been quite manageable, stood straight up from her head like a porcupine's quills; her tan colored skirt was ill-placed on her expansive waist; her T-shirt was worn inside out.

"Mother what would you like to eat?" I asked, gently.

"Some eggs and toast," she said in her low, deep voice.

"Okay. How would you like your eggs?"

"Scrambled. Butter the bread and fry it in the pan."

"Okay."

I quickly began to bring some order to the kitchen. I could not cook with it being so disheveled. I turned on the water to make dish water, while I placed the unused pots and pans back where they belonged.

"Mother, do you want this bacon?" I asked, pointing to the nearly burnt bacon cooking on the stove.

"Yeah, fry it hard. I like my bacon dark like my men," she said, matter-of-factly.

Mother was known to make such comments, but somehow they seemed out-of-place; like they should not be spoken by a person her age or in the condition that she was in mentally.

"Huh?" I turned to her as I laughed.

"You heard me!" She said with her eyes bulging from the sockets for more emphasis. "Bring the food to me in the den. I'm going to lay down."

"Okay," I replied.

I watched her as she used the table to support her as she stood.

"Mother, your skirt is crooked," I said.

"Hmm?" She asked, as she looked down at her skirt. "Oh," she replied, grabbing the skirt by the sides and twisted it on her hips.

No sooner than she had been in the den for five minutes, she called me again.

"Yes, ma'am?" I asked from the doorwell of the den.

"Bring me some aspirin. My hip is really cuttin' up this morning!" She bellowed.

"Okay."

I went to the bathroom and got the bottle of aspirin from the medicine cabinet. I poured Mother a glass of water and returned to the den.

"Here you go, Mother. Hold your hand out."

She held her hand out as I allowed two pills to fall from the bottle.

"I take three," she said, looking at me incredulously.

"Uhn hun, Mother. Three is too many. Plus, you haven't even eaten, yet," I said.

She looked at me and rolled her eyes.

"Here's some water for you to drink down the aspirin."

"Bring me a glass of Pepsi-Cola," she commanded, flatly.

"Mother, you can't take aspirin with Pepsi."

"Look, dag-gummit!" Dag-gummit was another way of saying gotdammit, but since she had become a Christian over fifty years ago, she refrained from using the actual terms. "If I want Pepsi-Cola, I want Pepsi-Cola!" She raged.

"Oh, Mother, quit actin' spoiled," I teased, jokingly.

She rolled her eyes at me again as she swallowed a very small sip of water.

"Mother, you didn't drink enough water," I admonished.

"Look, sucka, get out of here and get me something to eat!" She fumed.

I laughed at her as she gave me the glass from which she had drunk the water. I left the den to continue preparing her breakfast. A few short minutes later...

"Chris!"

"Yes, grandmother," I said in mock exasperation, after I had entered the den.

"Put my coffee in the mic," she commanded in reference to the microwave oven. "It's cold."

"Okay, but you know my name ain't Celie, don't you?" I said, referring to Whoopi Goldberg's overly accommodating character in the movie, *The Color Purple*.

"I don't care what yo' name is, warm my coffee!" Mother demanded.

"Yes, you're royal highness," I said as I bowed from the room.

I was eventually able to finish preparing Mother's breakfast. Our song and dance with one another continued for days into weeks and months. It seemed that I had come home from prison just as she needed someone to care for her. Despite Mother's stern demeanor, she was as gentle as a Lamb.

Although Mother was stricken with Alzheimer's, her beautiful spirit still shined through the debilitating disease. God in His infinite wisdom saw fit for me to return home from prison to someone whose enormous love of me would cover the hurt of having experienced the atrocities of being incarcerated and the woes and disappointments that came with being home.

Chapter Five

Change is difficult for many of us. The process of changing requires a particular mental fortitude and tenacity.

"Chris!" Tookie's familiar high-pitched voice pierced through the phone's receiver.

"Yeah! What's wrong?" I asked, quickly sitting upright in the chair of Mother's den.

"You know me and Todd been messing around, right?"

No, actually, I did not know that they were sexually intimate. I was not aware that they were even attracted to one another, let alone copulating. It was strange to think of Tookie and Todd being sexually intimate. Todd was Booger's best friend. They were raised alongside one another like brother and sister since they were kids, but I was not surprised. Stranger things had happened.

"No, I didn't…" I replied, nonchalantly.

"Well, yeah, we did!" She sounded excited.

"Okay…" I was interested in hearing what was the reason for the urgency in her voice.

"Anyway, you know he hustle, right?" Tookie asked,

rhetorically.

I did not know that Todd sold drugs; though, once again, I was not surprised. Although, he was White, he was raised in the hood. Quite naturally, the vices of the ghetto would affect him, too.

"Okay…"

"So, he asked me can he borrow some money, so he could re-coop." She stated in reference to Todd's desire to make more money.

"Okay..."

"You know me, cousin, I don't mind helping nobody! So, I told him I would give him the money when I got paid. So, when I got paid last Friday, I gave him some money and he said that he would pay me back the next day, but he ain't paid me back, yet! I keep calling him and asking for my money, but he keep saying he ain't got it! I'm trying to save my money so me and Lita can move!"

Tookie had a beautiful, generous spirit. She truly did. She would go out of her way to help anyone. She also had a wonderful work ethic. She worked under any circumstances: through sickness, death, and dire weather conditions. Although, her attributes far outweighed her negative characteristics, she still had a lot to learn.

"Hmm," I said, thoughtfully.

"Can you go over his house and make him give me back my money?" Tookie asked without hesitation.

I removed the phone from my ear and looked at it incredulously. Tookie had obviously fallen down and bumped her head really, really hard—several times. I did not know if I looked like Boo-Boo the Fool to her or what, but I had absolutely no intention of getting myself involved in some crap that was not my own. It only took one good knock on the head for me to have learned my lesson. And, I learned it! I had only been home from prison for a little over a month from having served seven and a half years for coming to her aid, for which someone's life had been violently taken, and she had the audacity to ask me to involve myself in senseless behavior again, because of money that she should have not loaned, anyway!

I was astounded. I absolutely could not believe that she would ask such a thing of me, after all that we and our family had gone through as a result of our previous actions.

Besides the sheer absurdity of her request, my elders had given me two rules concerning the loaning of money: never give money to someone who has no means of repaying the money; and, never loan more money than you can afford to lose. Tookie had broken both rules.

"Let me think about it," I said as I ended the call.

I did not return Tookie's call. I simply let the conversation dissolve as though it had never occurred. I was upset that she had called to enlist my help. I felt that the years that we had spent in prison meant nothing to Tookie; that the fact that I had taken someone's life, because of her initial actions, seemingly mattered very little to Tookie. I was hurt and disappointed in her. I wanted to believe that family protected one from hurt, harm, and danger; however, Tookie's behavior showed me that such was not always the case. Sadly, my experience with Tookie just one full month after my release from prison would be the first in a long line of lessons that I would learn about family and heartache.

I did not make a New Year's resolution. I had resolved years ago to always build upon the previous day's experiences and to make every day, week, month, and year better than the one before it. My one true ambition was to attend church service on the eve of New Year's Day. I needed to spend the New Year in the house of the Lord, thanking Him for His blessings as a new year replaced the old.

After accomplishing that feat, I began preparing for the new year. I looked at my to-do-list. I had promised myself that I would schedule medical and dental appointments upon my release from prison. Shortly after being home, I had gone to the Jobs and Family Services' Office to receive state-offered medical and dental insurance. It was imperative to me that I begin my journey-to-come physically healthy.

Although we inmates had access to medical and dental care while confined, the offered services were shoddy. Oftentimes the staff did not regard us as human beings, and the rendered care exemplified their mentalities. Our names were lie dormant on waiting lists for years before we would be called for simple dental cleanings. Major medical ailments, such as heart and lung conditions, were sometimes treated as if they were as insignificant as minor headaches.

My health had always been very important to me. With only one day into the New Year, I promptly scheduled a medical appointment to have myself thoroughly examined.

"Hi, Mr. Price. What are you here for?" A nurse asked pleasantly.

"Hi. I'm here for a general physical examination, but I'd like for it to be comprehensive. It's important that my cholesterol and blood sugar is tested. I'd also like a prostate examination and to be tested for HIV."

"Absolutely. How old are you, Mr. Price?"

"I'm twenty-eight."

"You know that you are a little too young to have any complications with your prostate, right? You look to be very healthy…I don't think you need to be examined for any prostate issues."

While I had a healthy respect for medical professionals, I did not like to hear naïve statements that were based on physical appearances. Diseases were not always apparent to the naked eye.

"Well, yes, I know that, generally, men are encouraged to begin testing when they are in their mid-thirties, but I also know that African Americans have a higher rate of incidence for developing prostate cancer than other ethnicities. For that reason, I'd like to be tested now." I said, resolutely.

"Okay. Sounds like you've done your research."

"Yes, I have," I said.

"Regarding an HIV test, is there any specific reason why you'd like to be tested? Have you practiced any risky sexual behaviors?"

"Yes, I have," I said, calmly.

"Okay, Mr. Price. Someone will be with you in a moment to draw your blood, so that the necessary test can be given."

"Thank you."

One week after my initial doctor's appointment, I received a phone call from the doctor's office.

"Hi, Mr. Price. This is Brittany at the Donaldson Clinic. Your test results have come back. We need for you to come into the office immediately."

"Okay. Is everything alright?"

"I'm sorry, Mr. Price. We are not at liberty to discuss any information over the phone. When is the soonest that you can come into the office?"

"I can be there at your next availability."

"Okay. How about…uh, let's see. Tomorrow at three?"

"Yes, that'll work."

"Thank you, Mr. Price. We'll see you then."

"Thank you," I said, as I pushed the end button on my cell phone.

I sat down on the bed in the guest bedroom of Mother's home. I did not know what to think of the phone call from the clinic. Obviously, something was detected in the blood that was drawn from me. I stared at the purple walls of the small bedroom, trying to ascertain what the call meant. The only thing that came to my mind was HIV.

I was taken to the inner rooms of the doctor's office shortly after I had arrived for my appointment. My back ached as I sat impatiently on the starchy, white paper covering the examination table. I arched my back to relieve the tension from my tired muscles, as I anxiously waited to hear the need for the urgency of the visit.

What had the test results revealed? Again, the only thing that I could think of was HIV. Somehow I had contracted the disease while I was confined. Although I was not promiscuous, I had had unprotected sex. One time was all that was necessary for an unsuspecting partner to transmit the virus to me.

During the bulk of my incarceration, I had been in two significant relationships: first with Moe-Moe and, then, with Michael. In addition to caring a great deal for both of them, I had chosen to enter the relationships with them in hopes of protecting myself against contracting any sexually transmitted disease. I knew that being in a faithful, monogamous relationship significantly reduced my chances of acquiring a STD. However, apparently, I was not cautious enough.

The wait was agonizing.

While I was not afraid of death, I could not handle being terminally ill. Aside from dying in a plane crash, I thought being sick was one of the worst ways to die. To live each day in pain as my vitality slithered away was unbearable.

Greater than my own fear was my concern for my family. How would they deal with my demise, especially from an illness as devastating as HIV? Could Mymomme endure another loss? She had already suffered so much already as a result of my incarceration. Surely, I thought, my death would claim her life as well.

"Mr. Price?" The doctor addressed as he entered the room.

"Yes," I said, as I stretched my back, again.

"As you are aware, your blood test has come back. Everything seemed fine, except there was a rather high reading of a protein in your body. I believe you have cancer. I am going to refer you to an oncologist, so that further tests can be taken."

I sat there numbly. *Cancer?* I had not considered that the prognosis could be related to cancer.

"Okay."

Strangely, I was somewhat relieved that the unknown threat was cancer and not HIV. Although both of the illnesses were equally as destructive, I did not want to succumb to HIV. I did not want to be yet another statistic in the African American or gay community. The stigma of having been incarcerated was enough to battle in one lifetime.

I also did not want my family to endure the shame of having me to die of HIV. Americans had not yet matured to see HIV as a disease that affects all people, regardless of the person's ethnicity, gender, socioeconomic status, or sexual orientation. Hetero-sexism clouded the thinking of most people. HIV was still seen as the gay disease; which, for many, translated to mean retribution and damnation for the gay victim.

Unlike my follow-up visit with the general practitioner, my appointment to see the oncologist was scheduled a full two weeks later. I calmly entered the doctor's office. I had come to accept the consequences of having cancer. I had found an inner peace, much like what I had experienced while I was incarcerated. I saw my life as a gift and that each day should be treasured as though it was my last day amongst the living. As such, I lived every day of the two weeks fruitfully. I did not party or drink, instead I did more of the usual things that I enjoyed: I took long walks alone, enjoying the beauty of nature; and, I spent more time with my family and friends, telling them, though also showing them, how much I loved them.

I had resided in the true presence of God during those two weeks. The Spirit had calmed and guided me toward a peaceful acceptance of life and death.

"Mr. Price," A white-coated man said as he entered the waiting room.

"Yes?" I responded, standing to my feet.

"Mr. Price, I am terribly sorry about this. I'm Dr. Whitmer," the doctor said in a rush. He seemed upset.

"Oh, it's not a problem at all," I said in reference to the long wait.

"No. I mean to say. You should not have been referred to our office," the doctor said, irritatingly.

"Oh?" I responded, quizzically.

"No. I reviewed your test results. Although the levels in your blood for a specific protein is higher than average, it is not cause for concern. While high levels of this protein do sometimes indicate cancerous cells, an examination of the other proteins shows that you are just fine. Each of us produces proteins in our bodies differently, though it does not mean that the production is indicative of cancer. The referring doctor should have known this! His behavior is entirely unethical! I am truly sorry for the inconvenience and stress all of this has undoubtedly caused," he expressed, empathically.

"It's okay. Thank you, doctor," I said, earnestly.

Dr. Whitmer and I shook hands before we parted. The general practitioner's prognosis appeared to be an act of mal-practice. However, my mind was far from his behavior and more on my blessing: the Creator had given me more time to spend with my family! I had not told anyone in my family about the possibility that I may have had cancer for fear that they would worry. With the threat having passed, I hurriedly pulled out my cell phone to rejoice about His favor with my best friend who just happened to also be my aunt.

"Geneeeeeeva, I love you!" I talk-sang into the phone after my aunt had answered.

"I love you, too, Chrissy-Boo!" She laughed as she talk-sang in response.

"Let me tell you what happened to me...." I laughed heartily into the phone receiver as I began to share the details of my experience.

Chapter Six

"Chile, you ain't got no friends dat you can introduce to me?" Ms. Maple, Leonard's mother, asked me in her warm, southern accent.

I was drawn to Ms. Maple like moths to light. Our camaraderie was somewhat of an unlikely occurrence, as she was far older than me, and she was also the mother of one of my best friends. In many ways, she reminded me of the women in my family: strong, fearless, and loving. She was a synthesis of Mama, Mother, Mymomme, and my aunts rolled into one person.

"I know this one guy, but you know he was locked up with me," I said.

"Chile, I know he was locked up! Dat's why I asked you if you know any men. I figure you had to a met some men in dere!"

"Uhn-huh…What kind of man you want?" I asked.

"Well, chile, you know I like young men! I mean, not young like you, but younger than me! And, you know I like'em big!"

I laughed. By big, Ms. Maple meant the size of the person's penis.

"Yeah, I know! And, they got to have a good head on dem!" I said in reference to their oral abilities.

"Uhn-huh, chile; otherwise, I don't want him!" Ms. Maple said, empathically.

"You know, I do have this one friend that lives in Lima. He's about your age, tall, slender, and his weeker-wacker is big…we had communal showers, so we inmates all had to shower together," I said before Ms. Maple had the opportunity to ask me how I knew about the size of his penis. "He ain't fine, but he is a cool dude with a really, really nice body. I didn't like him at first. He's from Mississippi and came to the institution talking a bunch a mess about women and punks—that's what they call gay guys in prison—all being alike and that we sneaky and always trying to trick a man so that we can get his money or penis!"

"Chile, sound like he crazy!" Ms. Maple said, suspiciously.

"He is! But not in that way. He was just talking mess to get a reaction out of me, 'cause you know how militant I can be and anti-sexist. He turned out to be a really cool dude, though."

"Whata name is, chile?" Ms. Maple asked.

"You won't believe this, his name is Roy Rogers!"

"Roy Rogers?! Like the cowboy, Roy Rogers?"

"Yeah," I laughed. "I told you he's from Mississippi, i.e. country!" I said, laughing.

~~~

After I had spoken to Roy about Ms. Maple, he asked that I give her his phone number. The two of them were like teenagers: they talked incessantly on the phone, sometimes late in the evenings into the early morning hours. Eventually, Roy drove up to Toledo from Lima, Ohio to meet Ms. Maple. They apparently liked one another enough to consummate their relationship. One weekend while Roy was visiting, I stopped by Ms. Maple's to see them.

"Mama, I don't want him here!" Pointing his finger at Roy, "You got to go!" Leonard fumed.

The smile on my face quickly faded as I entered the living room from the front porch.

"What's wrong?!" I asked, frantically.

"Chile, you is what's wrong! Done brought this man up in here!" Leonard rage, as he pointed in Roy's direction with his index finger.

"What?!" I asked, confusingly.

I looked back at my brother, Corey. He looked frightened, as he stood in the doorwell of the living room.

"You heard me! Done hooked Mama up with this man! Y'all don't know him from damn Adam!" Leonard roared, as he pranced around the living room like he was the Queen of the Nile.

"Leonard, shut the hell up! I can be with whoever I want to be wit!" Ms. Maple yelled.

I stood in the living room in shock. It was as though I had walked in on a war. I looked over to where Roy stood. His face wore a look of bewilderment.

> "That's the same shit you said about Carlos!" Leonard interjected, referring to Ms. Maple's second husband.

Leonard was very disrespectful toward Ms. Maple. He had no qualms about cursing in her presence, nor to her. He was also very protective and controlling of her. In part, the dynamics of their relationship could be attributed to the manner in which Ms. Maple reared him. She had given birth to Leonard and his two siblings at a young age. Although, Ms. Maple had married her children's father, the relationship was volatile. In the end, she left him. Without the support of a husband, Ms. Maple's parents assisted her in caring for her children. At times, I believe Leonard felt as though he was the parent. However, despite the circumstances of his upbringing, his disrespect of Ms. Maple was unacceptable. Ms. Maple was still his mother, no matter whatever her shortcomings may have been as a parent.

Ms. Maple looked stupefied for a moment before she retorted angrily, "That ain't none of yo damn business!"

Leonard's comment had wounded Ms. Maple. Her second failed marriage was disappointing and hurting to her. I felt sorry for her.

"Leonard, leave her alone! She's entitled to have a life, too!"

"You the damn reason he up in here!" Leonard said, turning his fury on me. "Y'all don't know him. His ass been in jail!" He shouted.

Most people seemed to have forgotten that I was in prison. They talked to me about ex-offenders as though I was not one of them. Their behavior reminded me of some White people's actions toward Blacks. Such Whites had no issue with talking to a Black person negatively about Black people, as if the person that they were talking to was not Black.

Black people are so loud...Blacks have such bad attitudes! It's like they're always angry...Black people really butcher the English language!

The White person's behavior was asinine; however, when Blacks conducted themselves in similar fashion, their conduct went far beyond idiocy, especially when it entailed discriminating against someone. How a people who had been enslaved and the victims of discrimination for hundreds of years could treat anyone with prejudice was beyond my understanding.

"He been in jail! What does that mean?!" I asked, angrily.

"It mean just what I said, y'all don't know shit about him! His ass could be a deranged killer and Mama bringing him up here around Dawn and Zulnell!" Leonard responded, referring to his nieces.

Leonard's concerns were legitimate. While, I had known Roy for several years, Leonard was not aware of the length of time or the extent of my friendship with Roy. In his mind, Roy may very well have been a serial killer. However, Leonard knew me; and, he should have known that I would not have introduced Roy to Ms. Maple if I had not known who Roy was as a person.

"What?! I know yo ass ain't talkin'! You the same nigga that see a damn stranger on the streets, chase his ass down, and then bring him home to fuck!" I exploded.

I was livid. Ordinarily, I did not curse in front of Ms. Maple, but Leonard's double standards had begun to wear on me. It seemed to me that he was trying to act as though he was concerned about the welfare of the household; when, judging by his own actions, he was not at all concerned about the people who entered and left the house when he was the perpetrator.

"Bitch, you act like you don't fuck!" He yelled, looking pass me and toward Corey for effect. "I know what you was doing in prison!"

I cared very little about what people thought of me and my actions. At sixteen years of age, I told my parents about my sexual and romantic attraction to males. Prior to, during, and definitely since that time, I had lived my life boldly, with little regard to what others thought of my personal choices. I was not ashamed of who I was or my experiences; however, I did not like that Leonard would use my younger brother as a pawn to upset or hurt me.

"Fool, you must be a gotdamn fool! I don't give a good gotdamn about what you think you know! You damn right I fucked in prison and I don't give a damn who knows it. Whatever I did and whoever I did it with, I can bet yo' mutha fuckin' ass, I wasn't in there being a hoe like yo' ass is out here!" I hissed, vehemently.

"Whatever, bitch!" He shouted as he rushed toward me with outstretched arms.

Leonard was big. At 5'11 and 200lbs., he was as large as a Zulu warrior in comparison to my 5'8, 155 lb. frame. He was heavily muscled, with the strength of an ox. Yet, in my overly-confident mind, he was no match for me. I quickly surmised that my small, muscular physique gave me the agility and speed of a cheetah and the strength of a grizzly bear.

I squatted low to the ground as his gorilla-sized legs quickly closed the distance between us with each step that he took. I maintained my position until he came within striking distance. I sprung up, forcefully pushing against the left side of his body. He stumbled to the right. I ran toward him, grabbed him by the legs, slamming him to the floor. I held him down, pinning him against the floor for a long moment before I released him.

Leonard huffed and puffed as he stood to his feet to charge at me, again. We repeated the entire farce until Ms. Maple intervened.

"Let him up, Chris!" She said between fits of laughter.

"Should I let you up, little lady?!" I asked him, mockingly.

He did not respond. He breathed laboriously beneath me. I released my hold on him and stood to my feet. Slowly, he began to stand.

"Bitch, you didn't do shit!" He shouted as he sucked in huge gulps of air. "We didn't throw no blows, bitch!"

"Well, come on, hoe! Let me give you what you lookin' fo!" I said as I stood in boxer's position to fight him.

"Naw, y'all stop it now! Y'all friends!" Ms. Maple yelled while simultaneously laughing.

"Look at you! You ain't shit! You sittin' up talkin to yo mama like she a alley cat! You fucked up! Look, yo' own Mama laughing at you!" I said, menacingly.

"Whatever, bitch!" Leonard said, tiredly.

"You got one more time to call me a bitch," I threatened.

The whole ordeal ended as quickly as it had begun. As usual whenever I had behaved stupidly, I was disappointed in myself. Although, I felt that Leonard was wrong for talking to Ms. Maple in the way that he had and for speaking of Roy and his circumstances as an ex-offender in a discriminatory manner, I should not have fought him. I had just been released from prison for having committed a violent offense against a person, and just a few short months after my release, I was involved in yet another violent offense—this time against my friend.

Although, Ms. Maple had delighted in my defense of her,

Leonard was her still son. I was wrong for having said vicious things to Leonard, let alone in his mother's presence and her home. For several years after our bout, the sting of my words would burn Leonard's soul. Until he and I mended our friendship, I felt that it was best for me to keep my distance from both of them.

~~~

Mymomme had somehow managed to purchase a car for herself. She was not working; nor was Sam. She did not say where she had gotten the money to afford a vehicle, and, I did not ask. After she acquired the car, she asked me if she could put the title and registration in my name, because her driver's license was suspended. Unaware of the legal and financial ramifications of allowing her to drive a car that was in my name, I willingly obliged; although, something in my spirit told me that all was not right.

"Mama, Mymomme asked me to put a car she bought in my name. What'll happen if she gets stopped by the police?" I asked into the phone receiver.

"Baby, you gone get in trouble, if they stop her. I can't believe that girl would ask you something like that. She know you tryin' to get yourself together and here she is askin' you to do some shit like that! Boy, I'm tellin' you the livin' truth! These kids of mine…" Mama replied, exasperatedly.

"Hmm, okay. That's what I thought. Thank you, Mama," I said as I prepared to disconnect the call.

"You welcome, baby. You gone put it in your name?" She asked in concern.

"No, ma'am."

"Good. That girl ain't have no business askin' you nothin' like that. These kids ain't gone never learn. Mm Mm Mm," she sighed.

"Okay. I'll talk to you later, Mama."

"Okay, baby. I love you, baby."

"I love you, too, Mama."

I disconnected the call with Mama and dialed Tookie's phone number. I did not disbelieve Mama, but I wanted to know exactly what the legal consequences would be if Mymomme was stopped by the police, or if she was involved in an accident. Tookie was not exactly street-wise, but she had more knowledge about such matters than I did.

I had long since moved passed Tookie's attempt to involve me in her situation with Todd. In order to survive mentally and emotionally, one had to continuously rid oneself of old rubbish and to forgive others just as often as the sun rises and sets, regardless of the pain he has suffered. I had learned to employ such wisdom while I was incarcerated. I soon learned that the knowledge I had gained while I was incarcerated was equally as necessary as a free man as it had been while I was confined.

"Tookie, Mymomme asked me to put a car that she bought in my name. She ain't got no license. What will happen if she is stopped by the police or gets in an accident?"

"They gone cite you, cause it's your car. They feel like, since it's your car, it's your responsibility. You know what I'm saying, cousin?" Tookie asked.

"Yeah, I know what you mean," I said, as I processed what

Tookie had shared with me.

After Tookie and I ended our phone call, I left Mother's house to go to Mama's. As I was en route, my cell phone rang.

"Hello," I said. The caller identification revealed that the call was from Mymomme.

"Hey. What's up?" She asked in a gruff tone.

"Hey. I don't feel comfortable putting the car in my name," I said, getting right to the point.

"Humpf," she replied with a snort-of-sorts. "I kinda figured you was gone say that. What your bitch ass daddy told you not to?" She responded, angrily.

Mymomme had always been incredibly possessive of me. Whenever she felt that someone was vying for my attention, she would go into a jealous rage. In times past, her jealousy had been directed at her sisters with whom I also shared a close relationship. As of late, her jealousy had been targeted toward my daddy and my grandmothers.

"Mymomme, I'm headed over to Mama's. I don't have time for this stuff."

"Humpf, well, take yo' ass over yo' fat ass grandmammy's house, then!" She replied, hotly.

Unfortunately, Mymomme's tantrums were not news to me. I had been experiencing her rage-filled outburst for as long as I could remember. However, I had never known for Mama to be included in her anger. The inclusion of her mother as a subject of her disdain was a clear indication that she was continuing to unravel mentally.

"Okay, I'm hanging up the phone," I said, calmly.

"Humpf, and tell yo' other uppity ass grandmammy I said, hey," she managed to sinisterly spew into the phone before I ended the call.

My phone rang several more times, though I did not accept the phone calls. My unanswered calls gave Mymomme the perfect opportunity for her to vent her fury through voice messages. After she had finally exhausted herself and stopped calling, I listened to the messages. I was astounded. Message after message was filled with evil-spirited rants. The messages were essentially the same as our phone conversation; however, aside from the mean things that she said, the most hurtful aspect of the entire situation was that all of it occurred because of my refusal to place myself in a position whereby I might incur legal woes.

I shook my head from left to right as I again listened to message after message of bitterness and evil.

Welcome home, Chris, I thought as I erased the last of the recordings.

Chapter Seven

The day had finally come. The paperwork which allowed me to be paroled to Georgia was complete. In some ways, I was ecstatic about the move. I was truly ready to begin my life anew. I felt that my dreams were placed on hold in Toledo. I was not able to move forward in the way that I would have liked.

While, the transfer seemed promising in many ways, in other ways, it did not. I would be separated from my family in Ohio by six hundred miles. They, nor I, would have the ease of knowing that I was a phone call away from them.

Mother was still heavily dependent upon me. Without being made aware of my impending move to Georgia, for no apparent reason, she had begun to suffer from depression. She spent the bulk of her days in the den lying down on the sofa. She rarely talked and the only times that she rose from the sofa were to use the bathroom, which created another dilemma. More times than not, she would defecate or urinate on herself while trying to get to the bathroom. Pine-Sol and bleach had become my closest acquaintances, as I was constantly on my hands and knees cleaning a trail of watery stool or urine that began in the den continued through the dining room to the kitchen and ended in the bathroom.

Try as I did to get my family to understand the depth of her condition, my urgent pleas fell on deaf ears. Aunt Carol, Mother's second oldest child, was the only person who completely understood the total gravity of the situation. However, she was employed and could not be at Mother's home constantly to care for her.

A huge part of me felt that I should remain in Toledo to care for Mother, yet another part of me acknowledged the admonishment of my father to me when I was a teenager.

Son, you can't help anyone, unless you first help yourself.

I listened to the voice of my adolescence as I begrudgingly hoisted myself into my daddy's truck.

"Son, I just want you to have the opportunity to have a fair shot at succeeding. You can't do that in Toledo with everybody pulling on you for one reason or another," my daddy said as we entered Interstate 75 South.

"Yeah, I know, but I'm concerned about Mother."

"She'll be okay. Carol is there," he said, referring to his sister. "Let somebody else worry about that," he urged.

His words seemed calloused, as though we were talking about someone other than his mother. He did not appear to have any sympathy for her condition.

"Dad, there is no one there to care for her, but Aunt Carol, and she has to work. I keep trying to tell y'all that Mother is not the same woman that we have always known her to be. She doesn't cook, she forgets whether she's bathed or not, she just lies on the couch looking at the pictures of our family on the walls of the den. She needs someone to be with her at all times," I insisted.

"I would just rather that it's someone other than my son," he concluded.

From an emotional perspective, I was moved by my daddy's love and care for me; however, from a mental and spiritual vantage, his regard, or lack thereof, toward Mother seemed peculiar. It was as if he did not have the warm, fuzzy feelings that most people have toward their Mothers.

~~~

I had to admit it: I felt differently in Atlanta than I did in Toledo. As hard as I tried to convince myself that Atlanta was not the place for me and that I needed to be at home in Toledo, I loved the feeling of being in Atlanta. I felt invigorated and alive; like I could conquer my greatest fears and achieve my wildest dreams. My pulse seemed to beat with the rhythm of the city.

In addition to all of the things that Atlanta offered me, one of my best friends, Erin, lived there. Erin and I had been friends since we were sixteen. Our friendship was peculiar. It had its share of bumps and bruises, yet, despite them all, we had maintained our love and affection for one another.

"Erin?"

"Hey, girlllll!" Erin shouted into the phone.

"Erin…" I began.

"Chile, I know, I know…you don't like being called a girl!"

"Well, if you know, why do you insist on doing it?!" I asked, imploringly.

"'Cause, chile, I know it'a get your blood to boilin', honey!" Erin laughed.

Despite myself, I laughed along with him. Erin had a great sense of humor. It was his humor and his strength that first attracted me to him. He was the first male to ever hold the position as a flag twirler in a band at any high school in Toledo.

He would flamboyantly parade through the streets of Toledo, unashamed of his gayness in a city that openly deplored homosexuality. I saw an undeniable strength in Erin that reverberated with the fierceness of a blow horn on the Day of Atonement. Rarely was such courage exemplified in a person so young.

"Yeah, okay…I'm in Atlanta." I said, after we stopped laughing.

"Yay, bitch! I mean, chile! I forgot you don't like being called that eitha, honey!" He laughed, playfully. "Chile, we gone turn this city upside down! They ain't ready for me and my sister, honey! Uhn uhn, honey! These bitches ain't ready, chile, but they better be, bit--!!!" He said, excitedly, stopping himself from finishing the word.

"Where are you?" I asked, laughing at his excitement.

"Chile, I live in a loft in downtown Atlanta, honey!" Erin declared, pretentiously.

"Oh, excuse me!" I laughed, playfully.

"Chile, how those girls in Toledo doing, Ms. Leslie and Ms. Leeza?!"

"Leslie cool, but you know I haven't spoken to Leonard since we got into it at Ms. Maple's."

"Chile, you and that girl still ain't talking. Honey, y'all need to squash that shit! Y'all supposed to be sisters!" He encouraged.

"Yeah. I don't like what he said. And, I don't feel comfortable going over to see Ms. Maple's if me and Leonard ain't cool."

"Chile, whatever. Y'all too much for me. Giiir, I mean, chile…let me tell you about Ms. Leslie!" Erin said, excitedly.

Erin loved to gossip.

"What," I said, disinterestedly.

"Chile, you can't say nothing to Ms. Leslie."

"What is it about?" I asked, wonderingly.

"Uhn-uhn, chile, you got to promise you ain't gone say nothin' to her, 'cause she told me not to tell nobody, especially you."

"Huh? What's this about?" I asked.

Despite myself, my interest had begun to pique.

"Chile, you got to promise not to say nothing!" He insisted.

"Okay, okay, I promise! Now, what's going on?!" I asked.

"Chile, I don't know if I should tell you! You get ta actin' crazy when you mad…wanna fight and thangs!"

"Yeah, yeah, yeah, now, what you got to tell me…"

"Chile, Leslie had Marquis and I think she had Tommy, too!"

By 'had,' Erin meant that Leslie had been sexually intimate with them.

"What??" I asked in shock and disbelief.

Marquis and Tommy were my younger cousins. Leslie had known them since they were kids. It seemed strange for her to have been involved with someone whom she knew as a young child, especially someone as close as my relatives.

"I'm going to call him on the three-way to ask him."

"Chile, you said you wasn't gone say nothing!"

"Erin, you know that I can't not say anything! There's more at stake here and you know it!"

"Chile, I shouldna never opened my mouth."

"Uhn-huh, you're right. Hold on," I said as I clicked over to call Leslie on the three-way.

"Helllllo," Leslie sang into the phone.

"Hold on, Leslie. Let me click Erin in," I said.

"Okay, darling," Leslie replied.

"Erin?" I asked once I had successfully joined the call.

"Yeah, chile?!" Erin said, excitedly.

In truth, Erin wanted me to confront Leslie. Ever since we were teenagers, Erin had been a bit jealous of Leslie. He loved Leslie dearly, but he had always been envious of the attention Leslie received from men. I usually tried to stay out of their mess, but this recent news was a little too close to my heart.

"Hey, slut!" Leslie said playfully to Erin.

"Hey, Ms. Leslie, girl! Come on, chile, let's get this show going!" Erin said, excitedly.

"Erin, you are crazy…Leslie, did you have sex with Marquis and Tommy?" I asked without skipping a beat.

"Huh?" Leslie responded nervously. "Erin, you talk too much!"

"So you did?" I asked.

"Chile, they grown ass men now! Wit grown ass dicks!" Leslie responded, proudly.

"Leslie, you don't do no shit like that! They my cousins!" I said, angrily.

"Chile, like I said, they grown men now! You need to stop being so protective of yo' family!"

"What?! This ain't about being fuckin protective! This is my family! Out of all the niggas you could've fucked with, you gone fuck with my younger cousins!!! That's some stupid, crazy, ass shit!" I bellowed.

"Chris?" Sara, my step-mother, said from the doorwell of the basement stairs.

"Yes?" I asked, yelling toward the direction of the staircase.

I walked over to the staircase.

"We can hear you up here," Sara said, softly.

"Okay. Sorry," I said, lowering my voice. "I'm about to

go. I'll talk to y'all later," I said into the phone before I pushed the end call button.

I was still livid after I had disconnected the call. I could not believe Leslie. I did not think that she would ever do anything so selfish as to have sex with any of my family members, particularly those whom she had known since they were young children of five or six years of age and who were only eighteen and nineteen when the acts occurred. Additionally, there was a responsibility involved in engaging in homosexuality. Not everyone could handle the ramifications that resulted in homosexual relations, namely being ridiculed if the relationship was made known to others.

Chapter Eight

Being a parolee in Georgia was very different than being on parole in Ohio. As a Georgian parolee, I was placed on house arrest for six months, which entailed having a monitor placed on my ankle. The monitor had to be worn all day, every day and I was only allowed to leave home for work; yet, because I was unemployed, I was confined to the house for the entire day. Additionally, I was required to pay the monitoring company one hundred and twenty-eight dollars a week. Though, luckily for me, my daddy was willing to pay the fee until I was able to gain employment.

However, after weeks of confinement, my patience had worn thin. I felt like I was incarcerated, again. Though, perhaps, worse than that, my relationship with my daddy had become strained, to express mildly.

Although I had noticed peculiarities in my daddy's personality when he visited Toledo and during my short visits to Atlanta, while living with him I was able to experience the full cognition of who he had become and how he had changed during the years of my confinement.

"I'on like that bitch!" My daddy declared, pausing before he continued. "And, that's what she is a dope-fiend bitch!"

"Hmmm," I responded, thoughtfully.

"Did I tell you what she did?" He asked.

"No, I don't think so," I said.

"Oh…We was over my mother's and at that time I think I was still living there…yea, 'cause that was right before me and Sara moved down to Atlanta. Yea, that's right. I had been putting up with her shit for months! You know she trifling! She leave shit everywhere! Hippie ass! Anyway, I was at my mother's and I went outside, and she got a bag full of cans in the front yard! Her crack head ass collecting cans and leaving them on my mother's front lawn!" He exhaled deeply in conclusion.

"And, that's why you're upset with her?" I asked, incredulously. Although his reason for being upset seemed somewhat legitimate, it hardly seemed enough to justify the depth of his animosity.

"Yeah…well, no…I just don't like her! She a dope fiend!" He exclaimed.

I understood my daddy's frustration with trash being left on the lawn. As a meticulous person, I knew that a bag filled with discarded cans would have bothered me as well. I also understood his feelings regarding her substance use. I intimately knew the havoc that chemically-dependent persons can have on the lives of those who love them.

However, conversely, I knew all too well that many people relegated substance users to a class of sub-humans. Such people failed to take into account that, regardless of the individual's status as a drug user, the person was still a human being and entitled to be treated as such, regardless of whether the person treated herself in a becoming manner in the minds of others.

Though what troubled me most about my daddy's behavior was,

unlike most people who harbored negative attitudes toward substance users, he had been employed as an addiction counselor. As a drug therapist, my daddy treated persons who were addicted to a wide array of substances. Consequently, he should have understood her condition from both a clinical and personal vantage, as he, too, had been chemically-dependent during his young adulthood—and, according to his own admission and the accounts of some of our family members, his addictive habits were far worse than the current victim of his tirade.

It was perturbing for me to hear him berating someone with whom he should have understood. However, most astonishing for me was that the person with whom he spoke so vehemently against was our family member.

"Dad, it doesn't bother you that you're saying all of this about your niece?" I asked, earnestly.

"Naw. Not at all. As far as I'm concerned, I ain't got nothing for her or Casha. They both are manipulative and self-serving! Casha act like somebody owe her something and Felicia is a crack-head ass, dope fiend," he conceded.

Casha was my daddy's other niece with whom he had negative feelings. Over the last several months, he had made me aware of the many people whom he had placed on "shuck," as he referred to the act of deliberately not speaking to someone.

As unhealthy as my daddy's personal relationships were, they were not by themselves an indication of the change that had taken place in him. He was also overly-occupied with the mundane. If he was not on the telephone talking to someone about Felicia or Casha, he was talking about one of his best friend's behavior. The majority of his days revolved around what other people were doing in their lives.

His slanderous behavior was unnerving to me, though life was not yet finished teaching me of the new person he had become.

"Sara, I'm going to Vegas for a few days. I'm meeting Carl over there." My daddy said to his wife.

"Oh? When are you going?" She asked, quizzically.

He looked up, pausing for a moment before answering her, "Wednesday," he responded slowly, as he assessed her question.

"Really?"

"Yeah, what's up?" He asked, uneasily.

"Today is Monday and you're just now telling me that you are leaving for out-of-town two days before you leave?" She questioned, rhetorically.

"What's the problem, Sara? Are you trying to start an argument with me?" He asked.

My daddy was not used to Sara questioning him. Generally, he did as he pleased and she went along with it.

"How would you like it if I suddenly announced that I was doing something without consulting you first?" Sara asked calmly, cornering him with her question.

He stammered a bit as he looked through the papers on the kitchen table. "What?" Pausing, "Did you pay the insurance on the cars?"

"Huh?" Sara asked, naively.

"Did you pay the car insurance?!" My daddy asked,

raising the volume in his voice.

"Uh, no, not yet…I forgot…"

"You forgot! How could you forget to pay the insurance?! I reminded you three times last week! Do I have to do everything around here, Sara?! Must I micro-manage everything in this house?!" He asked angrily before briskly exiting the kitchen, leaving Sara stupefied.

He had won. He had successfully manipulated the attention from himself to Sara and her oversight. She had unwittingly given him the ammunition that he sought to leave for Las Vegas without vindication.

~~~

"Son, you want to go see Dick Gregory with me?" My daddy asked one late summer morning in August.

I was curious to see and hear Dick Gregory. I knew very little about Mr. Gregory, other than what my daddy had told me about him, which probably constituted as a lot since he was always interjecting something into a conversation that Mr. Gregory had said.

My daddy's interest in Mr. Gregory bordered closely on an obsession. Framed pictures of Dick Gregory and him were hung all around his house. During my incarceration, he had sent me several photos that were taken of the two of them at Mr. Gregory's speaking engagements.

After my release from prison, as I visited our family members at their homes, I saw that he had sent many of them the same photos. Though, most interestingly, my daddy did not have a personal relationship with Mr. Gregory. They had never even had a conversation with one another. He had only seen and heard Mr. Gregory at his symposiums. He simply took the opportunity to take photos with him after the events.

"Yes," I responded, coolly.

I was eager to leave the confines of my imprisonment. I expertly ironed my shorts and shirt, laying them neatly on the bed until after I showered. After dressing, I met my daddy in the kitchen. He was dressed nicely in a suit and tie.

I looked down at my outfit: either I was underdressed or he was overdressed. I surmised that he was overdressed; after all, we were only going to hear Mr. Gregory speak. As far as I knew, it was an informal occasion. And, it was August. I would not have been caught dead in anything nearly as hot and suffocating as a suit during the heat of the Georgian summer.

We exited the house. As I walked to the passenger side of the truck, I felt as though I would faint from the stifling heat. Again, I was glad that I had chosen to wear shorts. We stopped at Target before getting on the highway to the symposium.

"Son, you're not going to cover up that thing?" My daddy said, pointing at my ankle.

I looked down at my shoe. The black monitor was strapped snuggly around my ankle in plain view.

"No," I replied, resolutely.

"You don't care if people see it?" He asked seriously.

"No, I don't. Why should I?" I asked.

"I don't know. I thought maybe you'd wear some pants over it, so that people wouldn't know that you were in prison."

"I don't care what people think. I was in prison; I can't escape that fact," I said, adamantly.

"I like to fake 'em out…" He said, suggestively.

"Not me. I don't give people that kind of power over me. What you see is what you get. I would be a fool to make myself uncomfortable in a pair of hot pants when I don't like the summer as is; especially just to make some people comfortable that I don't even know." I said as I walked quickly across the sun scorched parking lot toward the entrance of the store.

~~~

We were not in Target for long before we were back on the road. As was expected, our shopping was uneventful; no strange looks from the shoppers; no sudden outburst that an ex-felon was amongst them.

The drive to Georgia State University where Dick Gregory was speaking was awkward. I was irritated. I felt comfortable with who I was and where I had been. It was my daddy's prerogative to live his life deceiving people, if he so chose, but it was not all right for him to place his issues onto me.

"Chris, are you going to call the monitoring people?" My daddy asked.

My daddy had decided to list me as an employee of his within in social services business, which allowed me to be away from home.

"No. I'm getting tired of being on house arrest. I feel like I'm locked up again." I said, determinedly.

"Me and Sara will pay the fee for you," he offered, generously.

"I appreciate what you are doing for me, but it seems like a waste of money to me. Why should I, or you, have to pay for me to be confined?"

"You can enroll at Georgia State or one of the other universities here. I just don't want you to go back to Ohio. I feel like you will be sucked into the dysfunction of what's going on there."

My daddy had not understood my position. I had endured seven and one half years of absolute confinement. I did not like being in an environment where I had to be confined to a house. I did not like that I had to sit by a phone every few hours waiting for the monitors to confirm my whereabouts. I did not like that I could not sit in a bathtub, because the ankle monitor could not be submerged in water. I did not like that I could not take long, late night walks under a moonlit sky. And, most profoundly, I did not like that I had to depend on someone else for my sustenance; that is, my daddy and Sara's support to pay the exorbitant fees.

Atlanta had not been the land of milk and honey that I had dreamed it to be. Employment was no more bountiful in Atlanta than it was in Toledo. Despite being in a city where there were so many Blacks in positions of influence, ex-offenders still faced discrimination in the workplace. The only difference between Toledo and Atlanta in that regard was that, in Toledo, Whites denied ex-felons employment; in Atlanta, such an honor belonged to Blacks. For me, it was far more hurtful and disappointing to be discriminated against by someone who looked like me and shared my cultural history than it was to have someone who did not share those commonalities with me.

"I understand what you're saying, but I think I'm going back home. I can't take being under this sort of supervision any longer. I'll just enroll in college at Bowling Green or UT. The system here is too much like modern-day slavery. It's bad enough to have been locked-up, but to come home to more confinement is unbearable. These people are crazy," I said, waving my hand, dismissing Georgia's criminal justice system from my mind.

I continued, "And, the sad thing is that the ex-felons that received their convictions in this state have no choice but to accept these conditions. I can't take it…Plus, I spoke with Aunt Carol the other day and she said she needs me there to help with Mother."

My daddy was silent for the remainder of the ride. He said little to me at Dick Gregory's symposium and nothing to me on the ride home. I understood his desire to have me in Atlanta, but I needed to be where I was most happy. I had spent a great deal of my adult life being someplace where I did not want to be. It was time for me to live life on my own terms; to create the life that I had envisioned for myself.

I was outraged. My daddy had avoided speaking to me for two days. I could not believe that he could behave so immaturely as to not speak to me, because I wanted to go back to Toledo. I was further incensed that he would attempt to do to me that which he had done to so many others.

"Dad, are you okay?" I asked late into the second evening of his estrangement.

"Yeah, I'm cool," he responded, distantly.

I nearly laughed aloud at his level of maturity. It was obvious that something was bothering him, yet, rather than to acknowledge that he was upset, he had rather walk around the house acting as if I were invisible. He was not the same person who I had admired and respected for most of my life; whose footsteps in which I had attempted to place my feet.

"Are you upset with me?" I asked.

It was silly for two adults, who were supposedly mature individuals, not to communicate about whatever bothered them.

He turned his head slightly in the direction of where I stood in kitchen. "Yeah, I'm upset that I brought you down here, paid for your monitoring fees, and you have the nerve to disrespect me by waving me off!"

"What?" I asked, looking at him unbelievingly. "What are you talking about? I told you many times how much I appreciate all that you and Sara have done for me: welcoming me into your home, providing food for me here in your residence as well as the many restaurants where you have paid for me to eat, for allowing me to shower and rest in a clean, comfortable home! Why would you say that? And, when did I wave you off?!" I asked, perplexingly.

"When we were in the truck talking about your house arrest..." He replied, unable, within good conscious, to respond to any of the other things that I had previously expressed.

I diligently searched my memory trying to remember to what he was referring. With lightning speed, I mentally reviewed the sequence of events that day.

"Are you talking about when I said that I was tired of the being on house arrest?" I waited for him to acknowledge my question affirmatively, once he did, I proceeded. "I waved my hand in rejection of them, the monitoring people, the slave-like conditions of the criminal justice system here; I was dismissing their rules from my mind, not you!" I said, angrily. The more I thought about his childish attitude, the more upset I became. "I wouldn't disrespect you like that! You hadn't done anything to me! You and Sara have been nothing, but good to me! Why would I do something so stupid?!" I asked, bewilderingly.

I had lost control. My voice had risen with each sentence. I looked at him as he stood at the kitchen sink. He fumbled with dishes, trying to avoid my glare. I had enough. I turned from him without saying a word more and walked downstairs to the basement to pack my belongings. I would not allow him to treat me like I had committed some great sin. This 'shuck' thing gave him way too much power and control. At a moment's whim, he would stop communicating with someone because of what he perceived as a wrong doing. When judging by his actions since I had been home, it was he who needed to be placed on shuck by many people, not just by one person. He could have his immature mentality, but he would not have it with me.

After I had finished packing, I called my cousin, Brandy, and asked her to come to get me. She willingly obliged.

Brandy had gotten married the previous year. She and her

husband had recently moved to the south side of Atlanta. They graciously allowed me to stay with them until I went back home to Toledo.

~~~

Karen drove up to Atlanta from Macon, Georgia. At her insistence, I chose to spend a few days with her before I made the voyage back to Toledo. The drive to Macon, where Karen lived, was only an hour south from Brandy's place.

"Well, this is it?" Karen smiled as we exited her car.

I looked around the apartment complex. It reminded me of the apartments in Atlanta.

"This is nice," I said after briefly surveying the land from where I stood.

"Yeah. There is a pool over there and I think there's a tennis court around here. I don't play, so I don't know where it is," Karen smiled, sweetly. "Come on. Let's go inside," she encouraged, excitedly.

I followed Karen into her two-bedroom apartment. As was the case with the exterior of the apartment, the interior was pleasant.

"This is Angel's room," Karen said, pointing in the direction of her daughter's room. "And, this is where we'll be sleeping," she smiled, mischievously.

Hours later, we began to prepare to go to sleep. I moved to the right side of the bed, sensing that she probably slept on the other side near the alarm clock. I generally slept naked, but, because I was not sleeping alone, I kept on my underwear.

Karen entered the bedroom from the bathroom in her bra and panties. It had been a long time since I had seen a woman's body. She had gained a little weight, though not much, especially considering eight years had passed and she now had a young child. Her body still looked as exquisite as it had when we were younger. Before getting into to the bed, Karen turned off the light and unfastened her bra, exposing her breast. Even in the dark, I could see her breasts pendulously moving from side to side as she stepped into the bed. She snuggled against me. Her body was warm and soft. For a fleeting moment, I remembered what it was like to make love with her. I remembered the softness of her vaginal walls; the way that she arched her back, inviting me to enter her more deeply.

I consciously shook the memory from my mind. Karen turned to kiss me. I moved my head ever so slightly.

"What's wrong? You don't like me anymore?" Karen asked with a trace of hurt in her voice.

"Nothing's wrong. I just think that we still need more time to get to know one another," I replied.

"But don't you find me appealing?" Karen asked in a seductive voice. Her breast rested against my abdomen, as she slid off her panties, seemingly in one movement.

"Of course, I do, but we still need to get to know one another," I said, gently moving away from her.

"Oh," she replied dejectedly, shifting her body onto her right shoulder, turning her back to me.

I did not mean to hurt her feelings; however, I was not yet ready to have sex. I had had *simply* sex many times in my life. I did not want to embark upon a sexual escapade with Karen or anyone. The next time that I had sex with someone I wanted it to mean something beyond only two bodies connecting for a brief moment until we climaxed. I wanted for us to mean something to one another afterwards.

"You know, if you want, you can work-out with me from time to time," I said, unthinkingly attempting to change the subject. I should have chosen a different subject.

"I don't need to lose weight!" Karen said slightly rising from the bed. "I'm fine with my body the way it is."

"I didn't mean it like that…I was just saying you can, if you want to. I'm always trying to encourage people to exercise to stay healthy." I said, truthfully. However, my statement fell on deaf ears.

"I know plenty of men who love my body!" Karen expressed, angrily.

"Karen, I was not saying that there is anything wrong with your body! Your body is beautiful! I was just making a statement!" I said, imploringly.

There was no use in trying to get her to understand that I meant no harm. She already had it set in her mind that I was being mean to her. I should have known better than to talk to her about a sensitive subject as exercising while she was naked, and after she had just made a sexual advance toward me. Her body had always been a tool that attracted the attention of men. For me to seemingly reject her and to talk about exercising in the next sentence was akin to a slap on the face. I was not thinking.

I had pushed the previous night's events into the recesses of mind. I fully understood how my words and actions could have been construed as mean and insensitive, though after apologizing and explaining that I meant no harm, I thought the situation should have dissolved from our minds. Karen did not think the same way as I did, however. From the moment that I opened my eyes and looked into hers, I knew that I was in for a ride. Her face was contorted in a grimace that only Jesus could fix.

She held onto her foul disposition long after we had left her apartment; until finally, her mind could no longer handle whatever duress it had conjured.

"I don't have to take this shit!" She declared without warning.

"What are you talking about?" I asked, laughed at her unexpected outburst.

I had a knack of choosing the most inappropriate times to laugh. I could not help myself. Whenever I witnessed someone acting bizarrely (or crazy as I called it), I erupted in laughter. However, my laughter usually made the situations worse.

"Uhn uh, you got to go! I'm not going through this shit with you niggas!" She raged.

"What is wrong with you?" I asked through unveiled laughter. "You can't seriously still be mad, because of what I said last night."

"Either I'm going to let you off right here or I'ma take you to the bus station," she hissed, vehemently.

"You need a therapist. I DID NOT MEAN ANY HARM WHEN I MADE THE COMMENT ABOUT EXERCISING!" I said, deliberately enunciating each of the words for clarification. Though, she still looked as though she had a stick lodged between the walls of her rectum. "Yo' ass is still crazy as hell. Some things never change!" I said, shaking my head from left to right. "You can let me off right here. I'll find my way to where I need to go."

And, just like that, Karen swerved her car to the right of the road, abruptly stopping at the curb. I quickly grabbed my bag and exited the car, never to see her, again.

Chapter Nine

"Thank you for coming to get me, cousin," I said to Tookie as I leaned over the middle console of the car to hug her.

"Fa sho, cousin. You know how we do it," Tookie responded, sincerely.

Booger moved from the rear of the car to sit in the front passenger seat.

"Thank you, cousin." I said, hugging him firmly as we passed one another.

"Aww, it ain't nothing," he replied, coolly.

I truly valued Booger and Tookie. At a moment's notice, they had stopped everything to come to get me 600 miles away. Familial relationships, like life, were filled with highs and lows. Although my relationship with Tookie had come with painful lessons, our relationship was the perfect example of love and its redemptive power.

~~~~~

As I opened the door to Mother's home, a strong odor hit me. The stench smelled similar to that of a mismanaged nursing home. I placed my luggage down near the front door. Mother's bedroom was adjacent to the living room. I walked toward her room. The sound of snoring was audible long before I had even placed a foot into her bedroom. I looked at my watch: 11:37 A.M.

"Mother?" I whispered, as I entered her bedroom.

Mother adjusted her eyes for a long moment before she responded.

"Chris?"

"Yes," I smiled.

"Hey, doll!"

I smiled more broadly. I was pleased that she remembered me. I feared that she would not know who I was when I returned home.

"How have you been?" I asked as I leaned down to hug her.

"I been okay," she said in a low, husky voice. "I missed you."

"I missed you, too," I said, smiling, again. "Why are you still in bed?"

"I don't know," she said, looking away. "What time is it?"

"It's almost twelve noon," I responded.

"What!" She exclaimed astonishingly as she began to stir from the bed.

"Yes," I laughed aloud. She moved quickly as though she had a hot date in which she was late. "Are you hungry?" I asked as I began to walk from her bedroom to give her privacy while she dressed.

"No, I'm fine."

I went to the kitchen to make a pot of coffee for her. She always liked to begin her day with a cup of rich coffee with an ample amount of sugar. I looked in the refrigerator for something to give her as a snack to take her medication.

Moments later, she emerged from her bedroom dressed in her infamous tan skirt and a T-shirt. The T-shirt was placed on backwards and her shoes were on the wrong feet.

"Mother, your shirt is on backwards," I announced.

"Huh?"

"Your T-shirt is on backward. See? The tag is in the front," I said as I pulled the front of her shirt, so that she could see the label.

"Oh, I didn't even know."

"Step into your bedroom and turn it around. Do you need any help?"

"Naw, I got it," she said, retracing her footsteps from the dining room back into her bedroom.

I found a fruit cup in the refrigerator. I placed it on the dining room table, poured the contents into a small bowl, and added a little sugar to it. Mother would not eat it from the container, nor would she eat it without more sugar. She exited her bedroom just as I was coming out of the kitchen. She had successfully turned around her shirt correctly.

"Grandmother, sit down in the den so that I can put your shoes on the right foot and give you your medication," I instructed.

"Huh?"

"Your shoes are on the wrong foot and you've got to take your medication."

"Oh."

She sat down in a one of the two green chairs in the den.

"Let me see your foot," I asked as I squatted down.

I took her shoes off and placed them on her feet correctly.

"Here you are." I placed a dinner tray in front of her with the fruit and a napkin on it.

"What's that?" She asked, uninterestingly.

"Some mixed fruit. You need to take your medication and you can't take it on an empty stomach," I coaxed.

I had to choose my words wisely and gently. I had to be insistent, yet not too authoritative, or she would not eat. She could be incredibly stubborn when she wanted to be.

After she had eaten a couple spoonfuls of the fruit, I gave her the medication. Aunt Carol had placed the medication in a blue container with the days of the week labeled across the top and the number of doses to take each day.

"What's that for?" She asked as I gave her the pills.

"That pill is for your memory; that's a vitamin; that one is for your heart; and that one is for your nerves."

Mother's doctor had given her a prescription for antidepressants shortly before I had left for Atlanta. I mentioned to Aunt Carol that

Mother would lie on the sofa in the den all day. The antidepressants appeared to work. She sat up more often and had begun to read her Bible religiously, again.

"Oh," she responded as she threw her head back, tossing the pills in her mouth.

She reached for the glass of water that I had placed on the dinner tray. She swallowed twice, surprising me by drinking the water and two swallows of it. I had expected her to ask for her notorious Pepsi-Cola.

After urging her to eat more of the fruit, I took the tray into the kitchen, placing it on the table before I washed the dishes. I made my way to her bedroom. I had to tackle the stench that was coming from there.

I flipped on the light switch and raised the shade, so that I could see more clearly. I removed her cream-colored satin bedspread, pillow shams, and blanket from the bed. The pungent odor engulfed the room. I looked down at the linen on the bed. I was horrified. Several big, circular-shaped stains and a couple of other dark stains were on the linen. The larger stains were urine; the smaller, darker stains were remnants of watery stool. Mother drank so little water that her urine was the color of dark menstrual blood.

I made a mental note to myself to throw away all the mineral oil in the house. Mother used the oil as a laxative, though because of issues with her memory, she would forget that she drank it. She would drink the oil several times a day, unaware that she had already consumed far too much. The end result was evident in her soiled linen and underclothes.

I tossed the linen in a pile on the floor after I stripped the bed. The urine and stool had soaked clear through to the disposable liners on the mattress. It was obvious to me that her linen had not been changed in several days.

As I stooped to get the sheets from the floor, I saw the carpet in front of her bed was stained. I got down on my hands and knees to better see the stain. As I did, the odor from the carpet suffocated me.

Over the next several days, I worked tirelessly to get Mother's house back to the way it was before I had gone to Georgia. I cleaned the carpet and mopped the kitchen and bathroom floors. I dusted the tables and re-arranged the furniture in the living room and den to give the rooms a fresher feel.

The vast majority of our days were spent alone in each other's company. With the exception of Mother's close friends, Mr. Bill and Ms. Emma, she received few visitors. It pained me to watch her living her days virtually alone. When I was a child, Mother's home was constantly filled with people; family members and friends. Such people delighted in an opportunity to receive an invitation to attend one of her many lavish dinner parties or to simply bask in the glow of her humor and generosity; yet, when she herself could most benefit from a visit, few persons were present.

Feeling as though I could not tolerate Mother's near-isolation any longer, I began to reach out to my maternal family for support.

"Hello."

"Hey, Mama…"

"Hey, baby."

"Can I use your car tomorrow to take Mother to get something to eat?"

There was a long silence on the other end of the phone. Then, a huge intake of air, "I guess," Mama sighed deeply. "How long you be gone?"

"Not long, just a couple of hours. I just want to get her out of the house for a little while," I said.

"Okay," she sighed, again.

"All right. Thank you," I said, disconnecting the call.

After I had finished talking with Mama, I sat on my bed for a long moment thinking. Her hesitancy in allowing me to use her car troubled me. I felt uncomfortable asking things of people. In part, my discomfort came from my upbringing. Mymomme had instructed me as a child not to ask anyone for anything; if there was something that I needed, I should come to her or to acquire it on my own. The other part of my unease lied in the person's response to my request for help. There was always the possibility that, if the person granted the request, they would do so begrudgingly, as was the case with Mama.

I wondered if Mama was envious of the relationship that Mother and I shared. The thought that she could be jealous was mind-boggling to me. As a child and young adult, I had believed that adults were incapable of having such irrational thoughts and feelings. However, my experiences with my daddy and Mymomme had showed me that adults sometimes behaved just as immaturely as children.

While I was disappointed by Mama's attitude toward me asking to use her car, I had to admit to myself that she had always been particular about anyone driving any vehicle that she had ever owned, and with justifiable reasons. She was the mother of seven children and nine adult grandchildren. As such, someone was always asking something of her. After awhile, even those who were generous in spirit became weary of constantly being beseeched.

He was a distant memory of the past. Seven years had passed since we had last seen one another. As I watched him away walk from his fairly new car, old memories flooded my consciousness. His slue-footed gait was still the same; his smile still brightened his face, clouding the scars of his life.

"What's up, stranger?" He said smiling, as he walked up the stairs of Mother's front porch. How he knew I was released from prison and where I lived was no surprise to me—word traveled fast in small towns like Toledo—yet, how he knew that I would be at home and outside at that very moment was eerily odd. It was as though the cosmos had orchestrated our meeting.

"Not much. What's going on with you, Moe?" I asked.

He looked good. He had aged well; the years had given him a handsome maturity. His tall frame was still quite muscular, though not as bulky as it had been during our youth. Unintentionally, my mind traveled to our brief time in prison together as lovers. Our love-making was as passionate as our relationship was tumultuous. I recalled the smoothness of his skin against mine as though the memory occurred yesterday.

"Shit. How you like being home?" He asked, interrupting my reverie.

"It's cool. I'm glad to be out of Lima…just still trying to get used to being home. How long have you been home?"

"About two years…"

"Oh, wow, I didn't know it had been that long."

"Yeah, I stay out the way. Ain't shit out here in these streets, but trouble. Me and my girl got a place together…I'on do shit, but work and come home to her ass. She a good girl, though. I got lucky when I got her. We got a baby on the way. I hope it's a boy!" He exclaimed, excitedly.

"You seem happy," I smiled. "I'm glad you're doing well out here," I said, sincerely.

"Yeah. Who you stay here with?" He asked, changing subjects.

"My grandmother," I replied.

"This a nice house. Let me see what it look like on the inside."

Moe's request seemed strange. Although many people remarked on the beauty of Mother's house and were curious to see what it looked like inside, few of them were old lovers of mine and seldom, if ever, were the requests asked at nine o'clock in the evening.

"My grandmother is in there asleep," I responded.

"I'll be quiet."

I looked at him suspiciously. Something about his desire to see the interior of the house did not seem genuine.

"Come on," I said after a moment.

I opened both the security and front doors. The living room was dark. I dared not to turn on the light. Mother's bedroom was right off from the living room. I did not want to awaken her. I ushered him through the living room and into the dining room.

"This is the den," I said, pointing to the right of the dining room.

The old floors groaned beneath the carpet as we passed through the dining room and into the kitchen.

"This house big. How many bedrooms here?" Moe asked.

"Five, including Mother's bedroom down here," I answered.

"Yeah. This a big ass house. Don't look like it from outside. Let me see where you sleep."

Again, I looked at him suspiciously.

"I just want to see what yo' room look like," he said, sincerely.

Inviting an inmate to one's bunkbed or to his cell was an extension of friendship, just as inviting an acquaintance to his home in the free world is an offer of friendship. However, in prison, Moe's desire to see where I slept would have been commonplace; however, beyond the institutional walls, it seemed peculiar.

"Come on." I led the way up the stairs and down the long hallway to the bedroom that I occupied.

Almost immediately after entering the room, Moe pulled me to him. We tussled for a moment, until I effectively pushed him away from me.

"I ain't on that. Sex is the last thing on my mind," I said, sternly.

"So, what, you sayin'? You ain't had sex since you been home?!" Moe asked, astonishingly.

I laughed at the shock in his voice, "Naw, I haven't."

Upon being released from prison, the vast majority of ex-offenders drank as much alcohol as they could tolerate and they had sex with as many partners as they could find. I had absolutely no desire to imbibe or to have sex. They were distractions from what I needed to do to re-acclimate myself to my environment.

~~~

"Chris, you want to go apply for a apartment with me? This girl told me Owner's Management accepting application for rental properties on Dorr and in Bowling Green. They low income, too!" Tookie relayed the information in her typical lightning-speed speech.

I had not really considered having an apartment so soon after my release from prison. Yet, the idea of having a space of my own became more and more appealing as I thought about it. While I was in Atlanta, my cousin, Felicia, had moved in to help to care for Mother. Although Mother's five bedroom house was spacious, there was not really anywhere that I could go when I needed time to myself. Felicia's help with Mother would allow me to leave to spend a day or two at my apartment, if necessary.

"Yeah, when are you going?!" I asked, excitedly.

"This afternoon. We have to apply before everybody else, so we can make sure we get accepted," Tookie said, hurriedly.

"Okay. I'll be ready!"

Two days later, I received a phone call from Owner's Management. I had been approved for an apartment. I was thrilled! Just nine months after being released from prison, I was blessed with my own apartment. The apartment was located in Bowling Green, Ohio. Ironically, I had just applied to Bowling Green State University the previous week. The university was only twenty miles from Toledo. I was not only accepted to the university, but I also had been granted an academic scholarship, because of my scholastic achievements at the University of Findlay where I achieved an Associate's degree while I was confined.

~~~

I needed a car—and, quickly! I had grown weary of depending upon my family to use their vehicles. I was grateful for their generosity, but it just was not in my person to constantly ask someone to fulfill a need of mine. In addition to my own personal discomfort, I had to have my own means of getting to and from school in Bowling Green.

My plan was to continue living with and caring for Mother and to drive to school each day. During those times when I absolutely needed a break from everything, I would stay at my apartment in Bowling Green. The rent was income-based and, since I had no income, it was incredibly affordable. The apartment also gave me an additional sense of independence. I needed to feel as though I was supporting myself after having been so heavily dependent upon my family during my incarceration.

After several weeks of searching, I had finally found a car with which I was pleased. It was a black, four-door Grand Am. I unwisely used monies from student loans to help finance a down-payment for the vehicle; though, in the end, I had my own transportation.

Chapter Ten

Life was moving in the direction that I had planned during my incarceration. I had an apartment, I was enrolled in school, and I had begun to volunteer as a guest speaker. I first spoke at a juvenile detention center in Toledo. My brother, Miah-Miah, had been incarcerated at the detention center a few times. I felt that my personal experiences as an ex-offender would benefit the young incarcerates well.

I arrived at the institution early in the afternoon. I had chosen to wear a pair of dress slacks and a long-sleeved shirt to the event. Clive Jackson, the director of the program, greeted me at the front door of the institution just as I was exiting my car.

"How's it going, Mr. Jackson?" I said as I extended my hand to greet the older Black gentleman.

"I'm great, Mr. Price! Really glad that you could make it here. The boys could use a young, Black positive male to show them the way."

"The pleasure is all mine," I said, graciously.

Mr. Jackson escorted me through security and to a small room where a group of fifteen young guys congregated in various places in the room. They wore loose-fitting white jumpsuits. The sight of them in the jumpsuits startled me. I had expected to see them in civilian clothes. Seeing their young faces in garb traditionally reserved for adult offenders made me more aware of the reasons that I had come there.

"Okay, guys. This is the gentleman I told you about. His name is Christopher Price. Be respectful toward him. He has taken time out of his day to come here to speak to you," Mr. Jackson said, introducing me to the young men.

"Aww, man, I'on wanna hear this shit this nigga gotta say…man, I'm going back to my room…shit, I'm tired of havin' to listen to this dumb ass shit…" Several of the guys said aloud, openly expressing their displeasure with me being there.

Again, I was taken aback. Many days and nights during my incarceration, I had daydreamed about the opportunity to speak to young offenders about their wayward actions. I wanted to instill hope and positive change in them. I had expected them to welcome me. Yet, obviously, not everyone felt as I did about me being there.

"Listen, you will sit…sit down in your chair, Sanders!" Mr. Jackson said, irritatingly. "You will sit down and you will be courteous toward Mr. Price. If he tells me that any of you have been anything else, you will be reprimanded!"

The guys began to sit down in the chairs that were provided for them. A few still groaned in protest of being made to be there. After Mr. Jackson left, I began my spiel.

"My name is Christopher Price," I said from a position at the center of the room.

I looked around the room in the eyes of the attendees. *These are over-sized children*, I thought to myself. Many of them were bigger than me and with more facial hair than I would ever have in my lifetime, yet they were still children. Young people whom life had been unkind. Many of them were products of their environment: offspring of drug-addicted parents and impoverished communities. They resided amongst dilapidated homes, and educated in schools where the teachers thought little of them and less of their chances for success.

"I was recently released from prison after serving a seven year sentence for involuntary manslaughter. I don't want to lecture you and tell you many of the things that I'm sure you've already heard, but I do want you to know that you can change the course of your lives right now. You don't have to experience all that I have. You do not have to continue being separated from your family and friends, and the things that you love. You don't have to experience employers telling you that you cannot get a job, because you have a felony on your record. You don't have to continue living in the vicious cycle of your current environment. My life was just like many of yours. Both of my parents were addicted to drugs and my father was absent during most of my life. In between working twelve hour shifts and caring for five of my live-in cousins, my grandmother raised me. My younger brother and younger cousins were in and out of this very place where you all are now. Some of you may know them. You don't have to…"

"Man, I ain't gone keep hearin' this shit!" One of the guys said in anger.

My words had touched an intimate place within him. If I had been more mature, I would have capitalized on the moment, but I was not.

"What?!" I said angrily.

"Nigga, you heard me!" He said as he stood to his feet. His chair flew backwards from the force of his motion. His tall, burly frame heaved up and down as he breathed in and out in anger.

"You ain't puttin' no fear in nobody!" I said as I stood to my feet, staring him down. "I'm here to help you, not the other way around!"

"You ain't helping me. Yo' ass coulda stayed where you was at!"

"You need somebody to help you or else you wouldn't be up in here!"

"Man, Tommy, sit down, man! Dude came in here to help us and yo' ass actin' like a fool!"

"Man, fuck you!" Tommy said to the guy.

"It's cool," I said to the guy who attempted to de-escalate the situation. "He all right. You need to sit down!" I said to Tommy.

We locked eyes. My brows were knit together in anger. I refused to blink my eyes. I refused to give into his youthful tirade.

"Man, I'm sick of this shit!" Tommy grumbled as he grabbed his chair and sat down roughly.

Just as he sat down, Mr. Jackson opened the door to the room.

"Is everything all right?" Mr. Jackson asked in concern.

He had apparently seen the end of the fiasco through the windows of the room.

"Yes, everything's good. Thanks for having me."

"Man, see, what you did!" The guy in the front row turned around in his chair to say to Tommy. "Now, he leavin'! Man, you niggas don't appreciate shit!"

"Hey, hey, watch your mouth, Marshon!" Mr. Jackson said, reprimanding the guy.

"Man, thanks for coming, Mr. Price!" Marshon said.

"Thanks for having me," I turned to the other guys in attendance, "Thanks."

As I turned to walk from the room, I could hear the other guys berating Tommy for his behavior.

"Did everything go all right?" Mr. Jackson asked me once we were outside of the room.

"Yes, for the most part. One of the guys got upset, but everything was cool," I said.

"Okay," he said, hesitatingly. "Well, I'd like for you to meet Susan McDowell. She is the director of this facility."

Mr. Jackson and I walked over to where Ms. McDowell stood a few feet away from where we stood.

"Hi, Ms. McDowell. It's a pleasure to meet you."

"Thank you, Mr. Price. It's a pleasure having you here."

I smiled. "I will be in touch with you," I said to Mr. Jackson.

Mr. Jackson and I shook hands before I speedily left the facility. I needed to get out of there as quickly as possible. I was agitated. Although, I had managed to achieve some semblance of control after Tommy's outburst, a waging war was battling within me. I had allowed myself to lose control. While it was good that I remained strong during his antics, I failed to see that his antics were a cry for help. Because of my immaturity, I had missed an opportunity to effectively deal with Tommy's inner turmoil and to help release him from it.

~~~

I noticed that her abdomen had grown increasingly larger over the past few weeks. Of late, she had been unbuttoning her jeans as she washed dishes. Though, I thought nothing of it. I actually welcomed the sight of walking into Mother's kitchen and seeing her there with her pants slightly unfastened. Nostalgic memories flooded my mind: I pictured Mymomme deftly moving about the kitchen in her work uniform as she prepared a savory dinner. The thought warmed my heart with pleasant memories of my youth.

I had innocently assumed that her choice to unbutton her slacks as she cleaned was a woman's thing; something they did to relieve the stress of clothes that fit too snuggly. I knew full well that she was not pregnant, not at her age.

The first bit of news that something was terribly wrong with her came to me from my cousin, Autumn, later, her mother, Felicia, relayed the remaining dismal details.

"Little Chris, you heard about Carol?" Felicia asked me one dreary day in the spring.

"Yes, Autumn told me. What is she going to do?"

"I don't know. She has an appointment with an oncologist next week to determine what her options are."

"Oh, okay." I replied, sadly.

Hearing the details of Aunt Carol's condition seemed more real when Felicia conveyed them than they did when Autumn had initially shared them with me. I politely excused myself and briskly walked upstairs to my room, closing the door behind me. Alone in the room, I cried for a constant thirty minutes until my throat ached and my head throbbed. I could not believe that Aunt Carol had cancer. At twenty-nine years of age, no one in my family had ever been diagnosed with cancer; as such, I could not fathom what the diagnosis meant. *Would she die? Will they remove the cancer? Will she have chemotherapy?* My mind whirled in agony. It did not seem fair. In my naïve thinking, only the wicked in spirit were inflicted with terminal illnesses. I could not bear the thought of Aunt Carol's gentle spirit being gone from earth…and, so, I pushed any thought of her possible demise from my consciousness, until I had no other choice but to accept reality.

~~~

It was undeniable. I was in-love. The soft flutter of a butterfly's wings floated in my stomach at the mere thought of my love. The feeling of love had virtually consumed my every moment: passion-filled lovemaking sessions roused me from my sleep; I daydreamed while cleaning Mother's house; I doodled our names onto paper as I sat during lectures in class.

He was perfect in almost every way imaginable: kind, considerate, attentive, loving, and extremely good-looking. His muscled physique was coated in smooth, dark chocolate. He had nearly won my heart from the moment we met. Our first full conversation confirmed what I had felt in my soul upon our first meeting, we were kindred spirits. He was special.

The only problem: he was not in love with me. While he loved me deeply, he did not love me in the way that one loves a life-long partner or a romantic interest.

Michael and I met while I was incarcerated. We enjoyed a whirlwind romance for four years. Our relationship, like many relationships, was like a roller coaster ride filled with glorious highs and saddening lows.

The biggest assault to our relationship lied in the fact that Michael was not gay. While I believed that he truly loved me, he had become a victim of his circumstances; that is, he fell in love with me because he was incarcerated. If he had been in his natural environment, where women abounded plentifully, he very likely would not have been interested in me romantically or sexually.

Although I was hurt beyond what mere words could have articulated, I forced myself to accept that we were not meant to be lovers. The relationship met its end and, shortly thereafter, he was released from prison.

Yet, try as I did, I could not get him out of my spirit. I compared every potential partner that I met to him. As is the case with true love, most everyone fell short of what he represented to me in my heart, mind, and soul.

I had been home from prison for over a year and I had not been sexually intimate with anyone. I had met guys, but nothing came of the meetings. At times, I told myself that I was too busy with trying to become re-acclimated to my surroundings to entertain thoughts of a relationship. At other times, I told myself that I did not find anyone particularly appealing, which, in part, was true. The guys that I saw did not take care of themselves in the free world as well as they did in prison. Many of them wore over-sized, ill-fitting clothes and they did not groom their hair regularly.

Nearly everyone in prison seemed to be concerned about his appearance. Most of the guys worked-out or played some type of sport. Their clothes were meticulously ironed, and their hair was either freshly cut or neatly braided. In any case, they looked good.

While both reasons as to why I was not in a relationship were legitimate, they were excuses. In truth, I was in love with Michael and, in my heart of hearts, I was saving myself for him. While confined, Michael and I used to talk of a day when we would be released and how we would spend our lives together. I foolishly held onto those dreams until one day they came to a crashing halt.

"Hey, Mike," I said, as I tried to contain the excitement I felt from seeing him.

I stood up and began to walk down the stairs of Mother's front porch toward his vehicle.

"What's up." He responded dryly, hardly matching the exuberance of my voice.

His response to my salutation was not a question, but more of a reply.

"Not much. Just sitting around the house with Mother," I said, smiling as I climbed into his truck.

"Why you keep askin' me about these girls?!" He asked angrily, without warning.

The tone of his voice held a harshness and gruffness that I had never known to exist. My smile slid from my face.

"I'm trying to fuck this girl and you asking me all these damn questions! She lookin' all in my face tryin' to figure out who I'm on the phone wit' and what I'm talkin' about!" Michael said, exasperatedly.

My chest was wide open. My heart lay completely exposed. I was, perhaps, the most emotionally vulnerable that I had ever been with a guy. In a fraction of a second, the love and joy that I felt from seeing Michael and sharing space with him was gone. His words had reached deep within my soul and found my heart; with every syllable of each word, he sliced and shredded it to pieces, until the only thing that existed was the pain of losing someone that I had once loved with every extension of my being.

His love for me was gone. The truth was obvious in his tone, yet it was more apparent in what he revealed. Never would he have so chauvinistically expressed that he was in pursuit of sleeping with someone when we were romantically involved. He had no regard for me or my feelings for him.

"My fault," I managed to mumble.

He must have seen the pain on my face; the hurt in my voice. He stammered.

"I'm just saying…" He had begun to say.

I had already opened the door of his vehicle before he could finish his sentence.

"I'll see you," I said, solemnly.

My throat ached. My heart had descended to my abdomen. My feet felt like they were laden with lead. Each step toward Mother's house and up the stairs was laborious.

"A man, I didn't mean it like that!" He yelled from his truck.

The empty words hit my back and fell on the green outdoor carpet as I opened the wrought iron screen door of Mother's home. I closed the front door behind me and walked up the stairs to my bedroom in a daze of misery. For a long moment I sat on the twin-sized bed, until finally, I neatly sewed the pieces of my heart together and gently placed it on a shelf in my chest where I vowed to never let anyone hurt it again.

Chapter Eleven

The world to which I had been released was a very different place than the one I had left as a child of twenty years of age. While much of the physical world was the same, those who constituted my social world had altered. My family members with whom I was closest were not the kind, gentle, generous, and loving persons that they were prior to my incarceration.

In my mind, my world had become a science fiction movie where Martians had come to earth and seized the bodies of those most dearest to me. To make matters worse, not only was the behavior of my family different, but women, in general, were unlike they were when I had left home as a man-child.

I had come to understand that women and men were more like one another than they were unalike; women lied, they stole, they cheated, they killed, and they committed an entire host of hurtful things, just as men did.

For most of my life, I had believed that women were innately better than men. I had been raised in a household of strong, loving women. My maternal grandparents had seven children: six girls and one boy. I had a very special relationship with each of the women in my family. A large part of who I was as a man was because of the values that my mother, my grandmother, and my aunts had instilled me. I felt that any personal problem of women was because of something that men had done.

Mama, for example, awakened most every morning cursing and complaining before she went to work: yet, she was also married to Allen who had, in times past, physically fought her as though she was a man; that same husband had committed countless acts of infidelity with several of their children's babysitters and many of Mama's closest friends. The simple memory of such acts of betrayal and abuse would cause almost anyone to curse every morning and many times throughout day for the rest of her life.

Unknowingly, I had transferred the wholesome feelings that I had for the women in my family onto all women; while, consequently, I placed the unfavorable feelings that I had toward the men in their lives onto all men.

As a teenager and young adult, if I met a woman who had an unpleasant disposition, I assumed that a man in her past (or present) had done something to her to have caused her negative temperament. My ignorance of human beings as a whole would not allow me to conceive that the woman's cantankerous nature could have very well been the result of her own natural proclivities, not because of something that a man had done to her; simply stated, she was potentially mean-spirited because of who she was a person, though not because she had been scorned or mistreated by a man.

Because of my profound love of Mymomme, my grandmother, and my aunts, I viewed women as near-perfect as could be any human. As foolish as was my thinking, I had not allowed myself to believe that some women could be born with dark spirits, just as some men were simply mean-spirited individuals. As a result of my experiences with women after my release from prison, I was forced to see the larger picture regarding gender and gender relations.

Although I had been blessed with a broader mentality regarding the personhoods of men and women, my epiphany did not render me foolish. I was still fully aware that sometimes men were the cause of women's suffering: I knew full-well that men were the perpetuators of rape far more often than were women; I recognized that men were more often the abusers in romantic relationships than were women; and, I understood that, globally, men, because of our positions of power, were the cause of the world's contentions, including wars, racism, and, most profoundly, sexism. However, as a result of my broadened understanding, I had come to realize that women were capable of such unconscionable acts as well.

~~~

She was introduced to me as Janet. She was a pretty girl: smooth, German-chocolate brown-colored skin, evenly-distributed facial features, a radiantly bright smile, and a voluptuous body. I liked her as soon as I heard the first sentence fall from her mouth.

"Ohhh, who is this?" Janet asked flirtatiously as I entered the kitchen of Mother's home.

Corey replied, "This is my big brother, Chris."

"Hi," I said as I passed through the kitchen to the stairwell leading to the bedrooms upstairs.

"You want to be my boyfriend?" Janet asked, matter-of-factly.

"Sure," I laughed. "Give me a moment to tell Mother that you'll be moving in with us," I said wittingly as I ascended the stairs.

As I walked down the hallway toward my bedroom, I overheard Janet talking Corey.

"Your brother is fine! And, he sexy as hell!!! You see his arms and chest bulging through his shirt?!" She asked, earnestly.

I shook my head amusedly as I entered my bedroom. I had not truly considered anything that Janet said on that cold winter's evening. She was Corey's friend and, although she was older than him by several years, she was still too young for me to entertain seriously. However, as time progressed, I realized that beneath Janet's flirtatious behavior lied a very intelligent and loving young woman.

Within weeks of knowing one another, a friendship developed between us. I soon learned that Janet was the mother of a young daughter and that she was the oldest of four children. She had a wonderful work-ethic. She thought nothing of going to work every day as a home health care aide. She truly enjoyed doing what she did; caring for people.

Janet's parents were great as well: they had been married for over twenty years and had successfully raised their children in the love of God, as her father was the pastor of his own church.

For several weeks, my friendship with Janet flourished. We were not romantic partners, but I enjoyed getting to know her. In some ways, she reminded me of Mymomme, specifically her physical appearance and her candor. Her smile alone warmed my heart. She also had absolutely no reservations about saying how she felt or what she thought. I appreciated those qualities in her. I valued honesty and forthrightness in anyone.

Although I had maintained that we were only friends, Janet made it no secret that she was interested in copulating with me. Her actions were disturbing to me. I was not accustomed to women being so sexually forward. While experience had shown me that many guys were driven by their sexual desires, I did not expect women to behave as carnally as men. I held women to a higher standard.

When I had left home for prison, the vast majority of women that I met were very chaste. While, of course, there were some women who were promiscuous, most females respected their temples. However, many of the women whom I encountered after my release from prison were just as sex-crazed as many men.

Although I understood that as adults we were free to communicate our sexual needs openly and without reservation, I still expected women to conduct themselves becomingly. As children, we males were taught to value females; though, when females behaved in an unseemly manner, most men oftentimes resorted to treating them according to their behavior. In making themselves so readily available to men, respect for the female gender was compromised. I was of the opinion that true love and respect began with how we, as individuals, regarded our temples. If we allowed ourselves to be regarded as human dumptrucks, both from a receptive and insertive perspective, we communicated a lack of self-love and respect. With both genders being governed by our next sexual conquest or our pursuit of the ultimate orgasm, there was little hope of sanctity for future generations and their romantic relationships.

Times had indeed changed.

~~~

I walked into the sanctuary with the Spirit of God fixed firmly in my mind and spirit. I chose to worship in my usual section to the right of the pulpit. Placing my belongings on the seat, I kneeled to say a quick prayer of thanksgiving before I stood with the other parishioners, as we helped to usher in the presence of the Lord. I felt blessed in my spirit.

Church had always been my safe haven. As such, attending church was on high my to-do-list once I was released from prison. I had high hopes of worshipping in a free atmosphere, void of correctional officers. I had visited several churches in Toledo before I had finally settled on the church where many of my maternal family were members.

The church had recently appointed a new pastor. He was young, charismatic, and anointed by God. I loved to listen to him as he delivered the Word of God. I was so enthralled with the mission of the church that I attended Bible study on Wednesday and rose extra early on most Sundays to rejoice in the testimonies of the saints.

I had awakened Mother early that morning, prepared breakfast for her, and helped to get her dressed for service at her church. I escorted her to my cousin's car and watched from the doorwell as he drove away to take her to her church. Then, I ran up the stairs to get dressed myself.

I looked in the closet at the vast array of brightly colored suits and chose to wear a red one. Although red was my favorite color, it was a difficult color for men to wear well; too much of it or too bright of a red could look clownish. I chose to quiet the bold color of the suit by wearing a simple tie with the exact shade of red in the pattern as that of the suit.

My cousin, Robert (the same cousin who took Mother to church every Sunday morning), having seen that I was badly in need of church attire, donated the gently worn suits to me. After having the suits altered, one would have never known that the jacket and trousers were taken in several sizes to fit my small frame. The end results were impressive: the suits looked as though I had purchased them from a fine department store.

Slowly, in groups of two, three, or four, the saints began to enter the church. Morning testimonies had already been delivered; the praise team had led the way for the small choir to sing; tithes and offerings had been collected.

Pastor Brooks rose from his seat to present his sermon. He smiled broadly through evenly lined white teeth as he looked back at the choir.

"Amen! Amen! Y'all sang this morning! Amen! Amen!" Pastor Brooks declared, exuberantly.

I smiled and clapped my hands enthusiastically. The Spirit of God had rested upon the church. I felt like yelling in appreciation of God's presence and favor! He had seen me through every hardship and trial that I had ever faced: from prison to my dysfunctional familial relationships to my severed friendships. I had survived it all and was now able to worship God freely in spirit and in truth. I had come a mighty long way, and He had been with me during every step of my journey.

I looked toward the pulpit at the handsome pastor as he beamed from ear to ear. I was proud for him. He was just a couple of years older than me; and, yet, there he stood before a congregation of several hundred, rejoicing in the presence of the Most High. I did not know his journey; I was unaware of whatever past struggles he may have had, though I was immensely pleased for the young, Black man that God had chosen to lead us as children of God.

"Amen and amen," he shouted, again.

Pastor Brooks looked from the podium toward the congregation. He smiled joyfully as he scanned the seats and rows of church members and visitors who had come to worship God. Unceremoniously, he opened his Bible.

"Saints, I'm going to read from Job 42:10," Pastor Brooks announced.

The congregation stood at the reading of the Word of God. The book of Job was one of my favorite books of the Bible. In it, Job, a faithful and righteous servant of God, suffered unfathomable hardships for seemingly no reason at all. His children died; he lost his wealth; he was stricken with illness; and, his friends questioned his faithfulness to God. Yet, despite the atrocities that Job endured, he did not stop honoring God. In the end, because of Job's faithfulness, God blessed him with twice as much as he had lost before tragedy had fallen upon him.

"I know, many of y'all are just like me and you're wondering, 'when is God going to bless me!'" Pastor Brooks continued, "I mean, I have done the labor! I have worked hard! I have done what God has asked of me! I have lived an upstanding life like Job, so when am I going to get my blessing! I look around and I see the Devil blessing people with new Grand Ams and fancy houses! And, I wonder, when my blessing is going to come!"

I froze in my seat at the mention of people being 'blessed' by the Devil with Grand Ams. *Surely, he could not be referring to me, I thought?* Though, who else had recently acquired a Grand Am?

The remainder of the sermon was a blur to me. I was shocked. Perhaps, I was not the person whom Pastor Brooks had referred. *Maybe he was speaking in general, as some orators do. It had to be a trick of my mind. He was just using a Grand Am as an example to illustrate his point*, I thought to myself unconvincingly.

After church service had ended, I rushed home to check on

Mother and then I went to Mama's house to talk with her. Pastor Brooks was an invited speaker at one of the local churches and many of my family members and I had planned to attend the event.

"Hey, Grandmama," I greeted as I walked into Mama's house.

"Hey, baby. How you doin'?" Mama asked, warmly.

"I'm fine," I replied, taking a seat in the overstuffed leather chair.

"How is Mother Price doin'?" She asked in concern.

Mama had always thought fondly of Mother. Although, I still slightly suspected that she had envied the relationship that I shared with Mother, her questionable ill-feelings toward our relationship did not interfere with her true love of Mother. In some ways, Mama's affinity for Mother was rooted in Mother's age and her mental affliction. Mama's mother, Mother Reese, had passed away two years prior of complications from Alzheimer's. Mother Reese and Mother Price were about the same age. Subconsciously, I believe, Mama thought of Mother in the same way that she did Mother Reese. Aside from her association of Mother with her own mother, Mama genuinely liked Mother as a woman.

It was hard not to like Mother. She was such a strong, confident, courageously funny person. There were many times when Mother and I would go to Mama's house to visit and, as usual, Mother and I would playfully joust with one another verbally. Mama would sit on the sofa, nearly in tears from laughter.

"You tell him, Ms. Price!" Mama would yell from the sidelines.

Mother would look over in Mama's direction and wink her eye at her in appreciation of her support.

"She's okay. I just left the house. She had gotten out of her church clothes and was watching T.V. with her friend, Mr. Bill," I said.

"A mane?" Mama asked in southern dialect.

"Yes, he's a man, but he's just a friend. I already asked Mother if they were more than friends."

"And, what she say, C.P.?" Mama asked anxiously, referring to me by the initials in my name.

"She said she don't want no parts of no man and, especially, not Mr. Bill!" Mama and I laughed at Mother's straightforwardness.

"You goin' to go back to church this evening, baby?" Mama asked after we had finished laughing.

"Yes, I am…Mama, I think Pastor Brooks was talking about me today when he was preaching."

"Why you say that, baby?" She asked, earnestly.

"Because when he was preaching, he said something about the devil blessing people with Grand Ams," I replied.

"Aww, baby, that don't mean nothin'. He was just sayin' that. Sometimes I think he talkin' about me, too, but they say that's just how the Spirit work," Mama offered.

"Yeah, I know how the Spirit is, but that seemed liked it came from his flesh and was directed directly to me. I mean, why would he use a Grand Am as an example? That ain't no luxury car. I can see if he said something like a Cadillac or a Benz, but a Grand Am! Plus, I just got the car; no one else in the entire church has a Grand Am. I don't know, but it doesn't seem like a coincidence to me," I concluded.

"Well, I don't know either, baby. Just don't let it stop you from going to church."

~~~

Later that evening, Mama, Geneva, and I, along with a large group of our church members, accompanied Pastor Brooks as a guest speaker to the visiting church. Most everyone had changed from their Sunday morning clothes into a different set of clothes. I had chosen to wear another one of the suits that Robert had given me.

Pastor Brooks stood behind the podium in the small church. He looked radiant as he thanked his own congregation for coming to support him, then he turned to the pastor and the first lady of the church and thanked them for inviting him.

After Pastor Brooks had led the congregation in prayer, he introduced the topic of his sermon. The sermon was a repeat of the one that he had delivered earlier that day during the morning service. As was his usual, Pastor Brooks instructed us to open our Bibles to Job 42:10. His sermon was delivered nearly identically as it had been several hours earlier, with the exception of one modification: he did not mention a Grand Am.

"I know, many of y'all are just like me and you're wondering, 'when is God going to bless me!'" Pastor Brooks continued, "I mean, I have done the labor! I have worked hard! I have done what God has asked of me! I have lived an upstanding life like Job, so when am I going to get my blessing! I look around and I see the devil blessing people with new suits...."

My mind shut down at the mentioning of 'suits.' I did not hear anything else that was said by him. His mentioning that the devil had 'blessed' someone with a Grand Am of all cars was a direct indication to me that Pastor Brooks was referring to me; yet, I figured that I could have been wrong and, so, I attempted to place aside my suspicion. However, hearing him state that the devil had blessed people with new suits (and, I wore what appeared to others to be a new suit) was enough for me. I had dealt with such mentalities in the past. I did not attend church to experience the same jealous-hearted thinking that I had experienced in the world, especially when the attacks were coming from a pastor.

I attended several more church services at my family's church before I decided that I had enough of the pastor. I visited several more churches over the next few months, only to learn that the focus of many churches had changed during the years of my incarceration. Most churches no longer sought to positively influence the lives of their congregations; instead pastors preached what members wanted to hear, rather than what they needed to know and to learn. The goals of these churches lied in having their church services televised and collecting huge sums of money to build large, ostentatious sanctuaries. The superficial and vain needs of the pastors largely outweighed the needs of the parishioners. Many of these new-aged churches defiled the name of God and the cause of Christ. I was done.

~~~

I was between a rock and a hard place. My daddy had stopped talking to Corey. In some regard, I fully understood his reasons for discontinuing his communication with Corey. Yet, in other ways, I could not understand how a parent could stop speaking to his teenaged child.

"I don't like his ways." My daddy shared with me one day as we traveled in his truck on the familiar roads of Interstate 75 South toward Atlanta.

"Hmm," I responded thoughtfully.

"He's manipulative, self-serving, spoiled, and disrespectful." Continuing, "He calculates everything to get what he wants; he's just not a very likable person."

Dad was correct in his assessment of Corey as being calculating, though I did not know if he was manipulative. Corey was a thinker. It seemed to me that Corey thoroughly thought through situations to arrive at the best choice. His way of thinking was no different than the way that Dad and I deduced matters to arrive at a conclusion or choice.

I also understood why Dad felt that Corey was disrespectful. Corey was verbally challenging to the point of disrespect.

"For a long time, I did not refer to Dad by anything; not Dad; not his name; nothing." I shared with Corey and Autumn as we sat around the kitchen table at Mother's house late one evening.

"I don't believe you!" Corey said, indignantly.

I chuckled to ease the irritation that I felt from his remark and the manner that he had delivered it.

"I don't have to lie about something so stupid," I said evenly.

"Well, how did you ask for what you wanted?!" He asked challengingly.

"I simply walked up to him and asked or stated whatever was on my mind," I said, calmly.

"Nah, I don't believe you!"

I was not only perturbed by Corey's flagrant disbelief, but his tone also irritated me. He was a child of sixteen and, although I was his older brother and not his parent, I still felt that there was a more respectful a way for him to communicate his thoughts without blatantly expressing that he felt as though I was lying. I took great pride in being an honest person. For Corey, or anyone, to infer that I was being untruthful was upsetting to me.

As unsettling as Corey's ways may have been, I partially blamed Dad. As a parent, it was Dad's responsibility to attempt to correct Corey's actions, not to abandon him.

Dad had simply stopped communicating with him. He did not go to see Corey when visited in Toledo, nor did he answer any of his phone calls. Corey was deeply wounded by our father's severance of their relationship. Corey did not, nor could not, understand what he had done wrong. He, like me, wondered, *'what parent stops communicating with his teenaged child'*.

I tried to comfort Corey as best as could, though my efforts were in vain. Corey perceived me as Dad's favorite child. I believe that in some ways, Corey saw me as an enemy or, at the very least, as a constant reminder of what he did not have: Dad. He could not fathom that many of the things that he experienced with Dad had been experiences of mine as well. I shared with Corey countless memories of how Dad had made me feel as though I was not his biological child and that I did not deserve to have relationships with his side of our family. Yet, my attempts to help to heal Corey were in vain. He could only see the time that Dad and I shared at that present moment. His hurt would not allow his mind to see that we were allies in pain.

"My mom said she don't like you. She said you starting to remind her too much of your dad."

The words flowed from Autumn effortlessly, as if she was talking about disliking a particular food. I, however, was astounded. Her words hit me with the force of a herd of stampeding elephants.

As a child, Felicia had been one of my (S)heroes. I was enthralled with her educational achievements, her giving spirit, and her unique style of dress. She was the first person in my family to achieve a graduate degree of any kind, though specifically in social work. Helping others was not only her educational and occupational pursuit; it was her life's purpose. She selflessly helped anyone in need.

During Felicia's drug addicted years, she could be found at dining areas for homeless people collecting food to give to other people in need who were possibly ashamed to be seen at a dining center for the homeless. Her generous spirit could only be paralleled with her intellect. She was like a walking encyclopedia. She was able to converse about a number of subjects with the ease of a skilled surgeon and the wisdom of a tenured professor.

Felicia's choice in clothing was like no other. While my daddy thought of her taste as eccentric or hippish, to me, it represented her creativity and strength of character. In a culture where nearly everyone tried to look like people on television and movie screens, Felicia donned her colorful clothing as though Donna Karen herself had specifically designed them for her.

Quite naturally, I was taken aback by what Autumn shared with me. Although my daddy and I were alike in many, many ways, we were not the same person. There was little I could do about what Felicia thought or felt about me. I could not change her impression of me, nor was it a desire of mine. I had faith that, in time, she would see me for the person I was, rather than the person that her loathing of my father had created me to be in her mind.

~~~

My life had been on fast-forward since I had been released from prison. I had accomplished every goal that Tyler and I had daydreamed about while we were confined. My days, weeks, and months had consisted of school, working-out for five to six days a week, and caring for Mother—all while dealing with the stressfulness of dysfunctional familial relationships and friendships. I needed a break.

"Ludaaaa!" Brandy sang into the phone's receiver on one chilly winter day in January.

Many of my paternal family members had begun to refer to me by the nickname "Luda." The name had actually begun with Jared, Brandy's four year old son. Mistakenly, Jared thought that our family called me "Ludacris," when in actuality they were saying, "Little Chris." The misnomer was so infectious that it stayed with me.

"Hey dere!" I replied in the Floridian accent of my friends.

"What you doin'?"

"Nothing really; looking over some schoolwork."

"Aww, shoot! You go, boy! I'ma be like you when I grow up!" Brandy said, laughing.

"Aww, please, I'm tired of this stuff! I need a vacation!"

"You should go with us to South Beach."

"Who is us?" I asked.

"The girls…well, me, Marlise, Casha, and Janelle." Brandy said, referring to her best friend, our cousin, and, her niece.

"Okay," I said, considering her offer. "Where y'all staying?"

"Marlise got a room across the street from the beach. We all gone stay there. You can stay with us. I'm sure they won't mind."

"Hmm, okay. I'ma see what I can do. I've never been to Florida before, and Ms. Maple and them used to always talk about how nice it is," I said.

"Okay. Well, let me know."

I was excited. I wanted to go, but I did not have much money. I mentally calculated my monthly bills and how much I owed on them. After mentally putting some money toward each bill, I would have enough money for food while I was in Florida; that is, if I chose to go.

I called my daddy who said that he could get me a buddy pass through one of the airlines where his friend worked, so I did not have to worry about the expensive cost of a flight, and my cousin, Casha, had offered to buy me a couple of short outfits to wear while I was in Florida. Yet, despite nearly everything being covered, I still struggled with going to the exquisite coastal city.

I weighed the pros and cons of going several more times in mind before I settled on a decision. The largest con lied in me not have much money. It was not wise to go out of town with little to no money. What if something happened and I needed to get home?

The rational, conservative part of me said that I should stay at home. Then, I thought of all the years that I had spent in prison; years that I would never get back; years that I had missed spending time with my family.

I thought of how mundane my life was in Toledo. I rarely went to clubs, I did not drink, and I had yet to have sex since my release from prison. I needed to live, I told myself.

I heard Mother's anthem in my mind, 'Look, I don't drink, I don't smoke, and I don't gamble! I ought to have the things in life I want!'

With the conviction of my grandmother's declaration ringing loudly in my ear, I decided to go to South Beach, Florida!

~~~

Florida was beautiful. It was everything that I had heard it to be. I was sure that there were some downtrodden areas, just as there were in most major cities in America, though the small part that I was able to experience was exquisite.

Our hotel was located on Ocean Boulevard, directly across the street from the ocean. We simply had to step outside of the front entrance of the hotel and the ocean was right there! It was amazing to see the vast Atlantic Ocean as I took just a few short steps from the hotel! Ocean Boulevard was also lined with eateries and bars. I promised myself that I would live as though it was my last day on earth while I was there. And, I did!

For three complete days, my cousins and I awakened to the sound of the ocean at our doorstep. By noon, the sound of tourists roused us from our slumber. We dined on Ocean Boulevard after dressing for the day, and we drank ourselves to a drunken stupor during the afternoon, evening, and early morning hours! I had even shared a joint with my cannabis-smoking cousins; something I would have never done while matriculating in school at home in Toledo. Aside from its use being illegal, I was cautious of inhaling anything that would adversely affect my health or that would impede my work-out regimen.

My life was well-disciplined: I did not eat beef or pork, I ate three pieces of fruit every morning, I rarely ate fried foods, I drank a minimum of two liters of water each day, and I jogged four miles three days a week, in addition to my usual mile-run before I worked-out five to six days a week.

While in Ohio, I purchased a leather G-string, which I unashamedly wore to the beach. Never in my wildest dreams would I have dared anything so risqué. My style of dress was very conservative. I almost never wore anything that showed too much flesh. In South Beach, however, I placed my modest reservations aside.

The fourth and final day of our tropical excursion had arrived. We rode in the rental car to the airport in somber silence. Casha lit another joint to commemorate our experience in Florida. I declined an invitation to smoke the herb when it was passed my way. The festivities were over for me. It was time that I returned to my responsibilities in Ohio.

Perhaps, I had received a contact-high from inhaling the smoke of the marijuana in the cabin of the vehicle. I did not know. Possibly, in my own artistic way, I was honoring our time together in the tropical paradise. Again, I did not know. Though, suddenly the urge to recite a poem came upon me.

"Okay, y'all, I got a poem!" I said from my vantage in the front passenger seat as we drove over a bridge that crossed the Atlantic Ocean.

The suddenness of my declaration startled the ladies. Until my announcement, the cabin had been completely quiet.

"Oookay, Luda! Let's hear your poem!" Marlise encouraged, enthusiastically.

"Yeah, Luda, come on! Let's see what ya got!" Casha chimed in from behind me.

"Okay," I smiled, broadly. "The poem that I'm going to recite is written by my favorite author and poet, Maya Angelou! It's called 'Still I Rise.'" I said as I began to present the tone for the poem. "I used to recite this poem everyday while I was locked-up as a way of keeping myself motivated and grounded. Now, as I you listen to it, think of a negative experience you've had; think of an ex-lover who had done you wrong; think of someone who tried to hold you back; think of...."

Again, I did not know why I had the sudden compulsion to recite a poem. Though, at the time, it seemed completely appropriate for the moment. The need could have been inspired by the stillness of the miles of blue waters as we traversed them...Or, maybe the effects of the cannabis had penetrated its way to the fibers of my creative soul. I did not know; nor could I entirely explain why I felt the need to set the stage, per se, for the poem. However, in a small attempt to help my cousins to truly feel the verity of Angelou's words, I felt that a proper introduction was necessary; though not everyone agreed with me.

"Would you just tell the doggone poooooem?!!!!"

The question-demand reverberated in my ears from behind me like a siren, shattering the quiet ambiance of the moment. I quickly, instinctively turned around in my seat to face my assailant. Her once beautiful, peaceful face was contorted in anger and irritation. Her brows knit closely, her translucent skin had flushed a fiery-red, and the soft green of her eyes was barely visible.

I did not know what happened. Everything was so tranquil a moment prior. I had not stepped on Brandy's toes, nor had I called her, or any of the other ladies, the "B" word. I had not cheated on them, lied to them, or mistreated any of them in any way. Yet, my innocent action had caused my beloved cousin to transform into a demon from hell. I understood that my long-winded introduction of the poem could have been nerve-wrecking, though I did not feel that it deserved the attention that it received from her.

I disregarded the immense love I felt for her. My eyes only allowed me to see what I believed to be the devil incarnate. I had never seen someone so upset for no apparent reason at all! I inhaled deeply readying my voice to spew venomous words at my attacker. Yet, as I opened my mouth, I looked beyond the rage-filled countenance of Brandy and I saw a tenderness and purity beneath her demonic-looking exterior. Though her face was twisted in madness, her spirit was not. Time seemed to stand still for a moment. Quietness surrounded me. My mouth was agape, primed for attack. My heart pounded within my chest, forcing adrenaline throughout every area my body. I was armed and ready, yet slowly my mouth began to close; however, not for long.

"Yeah, Luda! Just tell the poem!" Casha retorted.

"Yeah, I don't see why you have to say all that extra stuff!" Marlise quipped.

I was snatched from oblivion. Sound returned to my ears. The reverie was broken. My eyes shifted from Brandy to Casha to Marlise.

"You shut up!" I yelled at Casha who looked as if I had physically struck her.

"And, you!" I turned to Marlise. "You ain't nothing but a follower! Everything Brandy say and do, you running behind her cosigning. You need to get a backbone and be your own woman!" I shouted.

I saw Brandy move from my peripheral. I quickly turned my head in her direction. She looked liked she did not like what I said to Marlise. I challenged her with my eyes, wanting her to say something.

"Y'all wasn't thinking of sayin' nothin' until y'all heard Brandy hoopin' and hollerin'!" I said lividly, as I turned around in my seat to face the road.

I was hurt. We had just enjoyed a beautiful time in an exquisite city in the nation and, within seconds, the entire energy had changed simply because I had chosen to offer a prelude before reciting a poem.

I was disappointed, not just because our time together had ended horribly, but also because Brandy's outburst was a common occurrence that was accepted naturally by most everyone who knew and loved her, particularly her friends.

Because of my naiveté, I was not aware that females, like males, operated from a hierarchal system—and, Brandy was clearly the leader.

While I loved Brandy tremendously and valued her intellect and her friendship, she was not my leader. I did not follow behind anyone. I was my own person, which is how I assumed the ladies thought of themselves, until that lesson in South Beach, Florida.

Chapter Twelve

I did not know who saw whom first. It was very possible that we both saw one another at the same time. Although, I doubted that was the case. He could spot a guy in the distance from two miles away from him. So, chances were, he saw me, without me being aware of him seeing me.

He sat in a chair on the other side of the classroom. Even from where I sat, I could see that his skin was beautiful. He was dark. Like South Carolinian or African-dark, as though he had been dipped in a pool of dark chocolate—not milk chocolate, but dark chocolate.

Our instructor asked us to stand in a circle and to introduce ourselves. Our class was large for a theater class, but small in comparison to other classes at Bowling Green State University. The group of twenty or so of us students rose to our feet and mentioned three things about ourselves.

He stood. He was tall and thin—extremely tall and extremely thin.

"Uhm, my name is Malcolm Mitchell. I'm originally from Detroit, and, uhm, I'm a sophomore," he said, awkwardly.

I smiled. I liked him. He seemed bashful, yet something told me that he was far from timid. Perhaps he was a little uncomfortable speaking in front of crowds, but he was not shy. His voice was very deep, which contrasted with his face. He looked like a boy, yet he had the voice of an adult man.

After we had all introduced ourselves, we played several games to get us comfortable with one another, though also as a means of enabling us to perform more freely onstage. Theater courses, as the one in which we were enrolled, dealt heavily with trust. As actors, we had to trust our cast mates. Unlike other jobs, the relationship between actors was different than that of co-workers in traditional jobs. Although co-workers in other careers depended upon one another to fulfill a job, the relationship with actors was more intimate. The dependence between actors was similar to a marriage in some ways. The actors had to achieve a connection or chemistry with one another; otherwise, the result could be disastrous for the production.

"So, where you from?" Malcolm asked as we exited the classroom.

"Toledo. How about you?" I asked.

"I'm from the 'D'!" He said, proudly.

"The 'D'! Oh, that's right! You're from Detroit," I said in mock sarcasm.

"You better know it!" He exclaimed.

"I should have known! I used to go to Detroit all the time as a kid. Detroit is like Toledo's backyard."

"Backyard?! I don't know about that! Maybe Toledo is Detroit's backyard!"

I laughed. "I didn't mean it like that. I meant because of the proximity between the two cities. We're only like forty-five minutes from one another."

"Ohhh, I was bout to say!" He said, laughing.

"What was you about to say?!" I asked, laughing with him.

Malcolm was cool. It was easy talking to him. It was as though we had known each other for far longer than an hour or two.

"So, what you call yourself having a crush on me?" I asked unexpectedly.

"Yeah, I guess," he laughed.

"What?!" I laughed.

I did not really expect him to be so forthright. That was another quality of his that I liked. He said whatever was on his mind without filtering it.

"I said, 'yeah'." He replied without hesitation.

It was apparent to me that he liked me. He smiled the entire time that we had been talking and he had a schoolgirl's giddiness about himself.

"Boy, you can't like me! I'm too old for you!"

"No, you not! How old are you?" He asked curiously.

I laughed. "I'm twenty-four," I said, jokingly. I was actually thirty-one.

"That's not too old. I'm nineteen."

"Nineteen! Damn, you look old for nineteen! I don't know what they puttin' in y'all food, but y'all need to leave it alone!" I said in humor.

In truth, he did not look old, yet he did not look as young as nineteen, either. His face was hairless, which made him appear youthful, yet there was something about his appearance that gave him the look of someone older. Maybe, it was his eyes. Unlike his flawless skin and his straight, white teeth, his eyes told a story that went beyond his nineteen years. His eyes conveyed that he had both seen and experienced things that exceeded his years in age.

"You need a ride home?" I asked as we crossed the street to the parking lot to where my car was located.

"Dang, we got here fast. I wasn't planning on walking you all the way to your car!"

"That's 'cause you like to talk!" I said jokingly.

He smiled good-humoredly at my jab.

"Sure," he replied in response to my invitation of a ride home.

～～～

The days passed swiftly. Malcolm and I had become good friends. Despite the difference in our age, we had several things in common: we were both born under the same zodiac sign of Leo, we had an insatiable desire of knowledge, and we were self-motivated individuals. Malcolm was double-majoring in international studies and political science. Not only was he very knowledgeable about world affairs, but he had an informed opinion about popular culture as well. We literally talked for hours, well into the wee hours of the morning, about virtually everything.

Despite his obvious attraction toward me, I had remained steadfast. I could not imagine being in a relationship with him. Contrary to the adage, age is far more than simply a number. A wealth of experiences separated us. I was twelve years older than him. I had been incarcerated for seven and a half years. I had experienced struggles and horrors that he could not fathom. Such experiences had given me wisdom that placed a greater gulf between us than even the years in our ages. Yet, despite my many admonishments, he still persisted.

"Hello?" I said into the phone receiver at nearly 3a.m. one Saturday morning.

"Uhh, can ou come ge' me?" Malcolm said through slurred speech, making it difficult to understand him.

"What?" I asked as I tried to better understand what he said.

"I staid, 'can ou come get me'?"

"You been drinkin'?"

"Yessss," he slurred.

"Where are you?"

"I'm, uhh, I'm at the…I'm at the student, uhh, union."

I exhaled sharply. "Okay, I'm on the way."

I drove as close to the Union as the streets allowed. Malcolm stood outside waiting. He could barely stand.

"Thank you for comin' ta get me," he slurred as he got into the car and closed the door.

"You're welcome. What have you been drinking?"

"Everythin!" He shouted.

I looked at him disapprovingly.

"Oh, sorry," Malcolm muttered.

"You don't have to apologize to me, but you need to consider what you're doing. Ain't nothing wrong with drinking and enjoying yourself, but you need to do it in moderation. It doesn't look good for you to be as drunk as you are and out here in the streets."

I did not mean to sound paternal, though I felt that I needed to tell him how he should conduct himself in public.

"I know. I'ma do betta," he slurred.

We arrived at my apartment in less than seven minutes. I walked into my bedroom and pulled my bedspread back as I got back into bed. Malcolm followed closely behind me. He laid down next me. I normally did not mind sharing my bed with anyone. I did not know if my lack of inhibition was from being raised in a large family and having to sleep with my cousins as a child or not, but it never occurred to me that allowing someone, other than a romantic partner, to sleep with me was inappropriate.

Within a few short few minutes of lying down, I had fallen into a deep slumber, when, suddenly, I was awakened by the touch of my penis being fondled.

"Uhn uh," I said to Malcolm. Through closed eyes, I moved his hands from my midsection, and drifted back to sleep.

Moments later, I was awakened again to Malcolm's head beneath the covers, preparing to perform fellatio on me.

"No!" I said, insistently.

"But, I love you!" He pleaded.

"You don't even know me to love me," I declared.

"I doooo," he whined as he attempted to grab my penis.

"No, you don't. Come on," I said, rising from the bed.

I walked to the other side of the bed and helped him out of it. With him staggering behind me, I escorted him to my second bedroom. The bedroom was bare with the exception of a desk and computer. I grabbed a couple of blankets from the linen closet.

"Here, you sleep in here," I said as I unfolded the blankets to make a pallet on the floor.

"Okay, I'll be good," Malcolm said through slurred speech.

"No, you won't. Good night," I said, as I exited the room and entered my bedroom.

No sooner than I had closed my eyes, he came back into my bedroom and attempted to get in the bed with me again. I firmly told him that he had to sleep in the other room. I did not remember why I had brought him to my apartment, rather than to his dorm room, but, whatever the reason, I had begun to regret it. Reluctantly, he went back into the bedroom. Hours later, I heard what I thought to be him vomiting, but I was so deeply asleep that I could not fully awaken to check on him.

I slept through the remainder of the morning, awakening shortly after noon. I walked into the bedroom to find Malcolm stirring from sleep.

"Good morning," I smiled down at him. He stirred from his position on the pallet. "How do you feel?"

"Oh, my God, I feel awful!" His voice was heavy and gravelly. He had a slight lisp to his speech, which was more evident in his hangover state.

I laughed. "Do you want something to eat or drink?" I offered, soothingly.

"No, I'm fine. Thank you…Oh, my God!!! I am so sorry!" He said with a startled look on his face. The events of the last night/early morning had begun to drift into his consciousness.

"It's okay," I smiled, understandingly.

"Oh, my God! I don't do stuff like that!" Malcolm nearly shouted ashamedly.

"Yes, you do!" I said, jokingly.

"Oh, my God!" Rising from the floor to fold the blankets, "No, I don't! I am so embarrassed."

"You don't have to worry about those. I can get them," I said in reference to the blankets.

"I made a mess. I'm sorry. I got it up the best way I could. I didn't know where you kept your cleaning stuff," he said, pointing down at a slightly visible stain on the carpet. "It didn't get on the blankets, though."

"It's okay. I'll clean it later."

"I can't believe I drank so much! I usually only drink vodka, but they had all this other stuff and I just kept drinking. I will never mix my liquors again!" He moaned.

I laughed. "You ought to drink a lot of water to flush your system and rehydrate your body," I suggested.

"Uhn uh, that's just go make me drunker! I'ma just let it wear off!" He exclaimed.

I laughed again. He was so dramatic. He said everything with passionate antics. "No, it won't!" I said, but I did not persist. He was going to do what he thought was best.

~~~

Slowly, my relationship with Malcolm drifted into a great friendship. Talking to Malcolm was easy. He was an attentive listener and offered great feedback. I should have enlisted the services of a professional therapist; yet, instead, I shared all of my personal woes with him.

We spent the bulk of our days together. I soon realized that his friendship was just what I needed. I was lonely. I had begun to spend less time in Toledo; the only exception being when I went to Toledo to clean Mother's home and to check on Aunt Carol, Mama and Allen. My aunt, Geneva, was so engrossed in chemical dependency that we rarely saw one another. Days into weeks would pass without me hearing a single word from her. She would later explain to me that crack-cocaine had her so far gone mentally that she was unable to wholly give anything of herself to anyone.

My relationship with Brandy was also different. After we arrived home from Florida, I had intentionally placed some distance between us. I needed to further process what had transpired between us there, but I also needed to better understand the person that she had become while I was away in prison. In itself, her outburst in Florida was minute, nothing that was really worth giving any importance; however, coupled with a few other oddities, her behavior made the event worth pondering.

Brandy had changed. In more ways than not, she was still the cousin that I had always known her to be; the kind and caring person that would help anyone in need. Though, in other ways, she was very different. She had become cantankerous and moody. Brandy had always been nervy, as I called her when we were children; which meant that anything and everything had the potential to easily bother her. Yet, of late, miniscule, trivial things had become more annoying to her: if a person showered for longer than she thought should be an allowable time to shower, she had something to negative to say; if someone placed pepper shakers to the left of salt shaker as opposed to the right, she had a reproach for the individual; when I referred to family members by their relation to me rather than by their names, Brandy became perturbed.

Brandy had also become short-tempered. She always seemed to be hollering at someone, no matter her relationship with the person. She was flippant with Aunt Carol, Mother, and, even our great-aunt, Hattie. She had begun to tell people that they were stupid or ignorant on a regular basis. I had a disdain for anyone being misnamed; however, when the names were used by a person as well-liked and loved as Brandy, the results were far more damaging. Her thoughts, opinions, and words mattered to people.

Such presumably insignificant actions may have been trivial if someone else had committed them, yet they were not for Brandy. She had always had a beautiful, welcoming spirit. People loved to be around her. Brandy's warm, soft green eyes and big, magnetic smile both tempered and drew the coldest of individuals into her sphere of love and acceptance. The blessing of her physical beauty, her intellect, and her gracious spirit were equal to none.

Brandy had begun to drink alcohol more often. Like many of us, she was battling her share of personal issues. She was a single mother and her fairytale relationship with her son's father had come to a crashing halt after she had learned that he was expecting a child by another woman. Perhaps, the demise of their relationship and the realities of life i.e., bills, unfulfilled educational and career aspirations were the reasons for the change in her personality. I was unsure as to the exact reasons of her behavior, however whatever the origins, her actions placed a strain on our relationship.

The complexities of my familial relationships made my friendship with Malcolm that much more endearing; however, not having healthy relationships with my family and friends also created an imbalance in my life, which would later result in poor decision-making.

~~~

It happened. I should have seen it coming, but, in all honesty, I did not. I thought that I had things under control. Yet, in the end, I had succumbed to my desires. Malcolm and I had sex. The sex was great. It was exactly what I would have imagined it to be, if I had imagined sex with Malcolm. But, I had not imagined sex with Malcolm. I did not want to have sex with him. Sure, I loved him wholly. He was a great guy and a great catch—for someone else, but not me. Yes, we had amazing chemistry. We loved being in each other's company. And, yes, he was beautiful, intelligent, personable, and funny—all the things that any person with good sense would dream of in a partner. But, he was not the person for me.

I was not ready to be in a relationship; I was not ready to be in-love. I loved too deeply. The person and the memories of the relationship stayed with me far too long, even after the relationship had ended. I had not fully healed from my relationship with Michael. I still thought of him; I still dreamed of him; and, unconsciously, I still compared other guys to him, including Malcolm.

Above anything else, Malcolm was too young. Although he was far more mature than most people his age, he was still immature in many ways. He truly embodied the mentality and motto of his generation: YOLO (you only live once). While I applauded his adventurous spirit, wisdom had shown me that not everything needs to be experienced.

"Have you ever been in a ménage `a trois? A three-some?" I asked Malcolm in regard to his sexual experiences.

"Yes," he replied, innocently.

"How many?"

"A few with my friends?"

"With your friends?!"

"Yea. We didn't do nothing to each other, but, me and Samay would have with another boy…Have you?"

"So, one of y'all would be kissing or licking on the dude, while the other one did something else?" He nodded his head affirmatively. "No, I haven't. I think I'm too possessive or territorial. Plus, I wouldn't want to lick where somebody else already had his mouth."

"How about drugs? Which ones have you done? I know you drink, of course!" I said, laughing.

"Mmm, weed, pills, ecstasy…"

"Wow, have you really? You aren't afraid of what they may do to your body; to your mind?"

He laughed. "No! I don't do them all the time, just when I go out or if I feel like having a good time. I'll try anything once!" He laughed.

Malcolm's generation reminded me a lot of my parents' era. It appeared that children born in the 1950s and 60s had rebelled against their parents' strict, conservative upbringing by having unbridled sex and experimenting with any drug that they could acquire.

Contrarily, my generation appeared to have been so ravaged by the choices of our parents' generation that we were more conservative with our sexual practices and use of drugs. While many members of my generation had indulged in substance use and exploratory sex, many of us engaged in them far more modestly than did my parents and Malcolm's generations.

Chapter Thirteen

Unseen forces are always at work in our lives; some of those forces work for our good, while others work to destroy us. Since I had been home from prison, the Holy Spirit had lovingly guided my steps and shielded me from unforeseen dangers. This time would be no exception...

We arrived at the San Francisco International Airport late in the afternoon. The sun sat high in the Californian sky, spreading its rays of light across its nearly cloudless horizon. The outside temperature did not feel like late-December at all, though that was part of the allurement of California, particularly the Bay Area, where the climate was moderate all-year around.

My daddy's fifty-first birthday was in a few days and he invited me to accompany him to San Francisco, a city neither of us had previously visited. I loved traveling, especially with my daddy. Despite our roller coaster ride-of-a relationship, I loved him and adored spending time with him.

While traversing through the sea of travelers, I was able to appreciate the sheer beauty and enormity of the airport's structure. It was so large that it resembled a dome where concerts or professional sports were played more so than an airport to me. In spite of the throngs of people, we navigated our way through the congested corridors with ease and great efficiency as we ascertained which train to catch to our hotel.

After arriving at our hotel, we ate and rested before we re-boarded the train to the city. We had no specific destination in mind. We just knew that we wanted to be in downtown San Francisco.

The train was crowded, though not so populous that we were not able to get a seat.

"Excuse me, can you tell me how to get to Market Street?" An Asian woman asked my daddy and me.

"I'm sorry, ma'am. I'm not quite certain. We are tourist ourselves," my daddy responded, pleasantly.

"Do you know if I'm on the right train?" She asked.

"I don't know. My son and I are headed to downtown San Francisco…" He shared.

"Yes, you're on the right train," an older White guy stated. "Where are you going?"

"Well, I'm trying to get to the Westin."

"Yeah, well, stay on this train until you get downtown. It'll take you right to Market."

"Thank you," she said, softly.

My daddy took the opportunity before him to ask the guy for directions as well.

"Excuse me, sir. My son and I are here visiting. He is considering attending graduate school in acting."

"Oh, there are few acting schools in the area. A couple of the better are ACT or the American Conservatory Theater and the Academy of Art University," the guy responded graciously.

"Thank you for that information. Are we on the right train to go to either of those schools?" My daddy asked.

"Well, yeah, both of them are in the heart of San Francisco. You just need to take this train to the F-line. Stick by me. We're getting off at the same stop."

"Thank you for your hospitality," my daddy expressed.

My daddy and the guy talked the entire time we were on the train. He was wealth of information. Not only did he give us an intensive history of the theatrical schools in the area, he also provided us with detailed information on the city of San Francisco as a whole, including major tourist attractions.

Just as the guy had instructed, my daddy and I exited the train with him. He walked alongside us for several blocks, and then pointed us in the direction of the schools. Looking through the crowd of people to the street signs, my daddy and I discussed which school we would visit first. As we turned to thank the guy for his help, he was gone. There was absolutely no sight of him anywhere. It was as though he appeared just to direct our way.

~~~

The world of acting kissed me passionately. I had happened upon the art a few months prior, when I had to take a few electives in order for me to graduate the following spring. The only available courses were in theater, so I enrolled in three classes: two in acting and one in film.

I had fully expected to be completely bored by the classes, however, I soon fell madly in-love with theater. My perception of acting centered largely on my gay friends' playful interpretations of famous movies, like *The Color Purple, Gone with the Wind,* or *Mommie Dearest.* I did not see the art-form in my friends' buffoonery; though, after studying acting, I realized its value.

Each of our lives told a story and within our individual stories were lessons. As an actor, I was able to entertain, inspire, and educate others by telling a character's story. I was ecstatic by my discovery. A whole new world had opened to me; a world where I could travel back in time or forward to the future or remain in present-day and use the gift of acting to encourage an audience to feel love, sorrow, compassion, joy, or understanding.

~~~

San Francisco was exquisite. Situated on miles and miles of rolling hills, the city offered the best of two extremes: city-living and small-town hospitality. San Francisco had the big-city feel of New York City; yet, it was void of the coldness and filth that was typically associated with metropolises.

Walking in the direction of where the guy had directed us, it was not long before we were standing in front of an amazing building. The architecture was astounding. Colorful banners were fixed alongside the huge columns of the building identifying it as, "The American Conservatory Theater: The Geary Theater."

I excitedly read of the upcoming productions that were posted in an encasement on the face of the building. I was in awe! I stepped back to look at the building and to better take in the city. I was pleasantly overwhelmed! The beautifully crafted buildings, the energy of the city, the schools, the trolley cars, and the majestic hills all filled me with delight!

I watched the scores of people walking determinedly along the streets to their destinations. I turned my head to the right, then to left, to the right, and then to the left, again. I was enthralled by the flow of human traffic. Looking at the passer-byes, I saw a thinly-built guy animatedly talking on the phone in front of the theater. I squinted to better focus my vision. The guy looked incredulously familiar.

"Dad, that guy looks like a teacher from Bowling Green," I said, tapping my daddy on the arm.

"Where, son?"

"That little guy over there on the phone. He looks just like this instructor named Mike Beak, but that can't be him," I said, as I instinctively began to walk near him.

I felt drawn to him as though being pulled by invisible strings. I was fully aware of movement around me, though sound had ceased to exist. I continued to walk slowly toward the guy.

I had heard it said that everyone has a twin, but I had yet to experience it. Though, maybe I would finally get the opportunity to see if there was truth to the adage.

I stood thirty feet from him. He walked in circles as he continued to talk ardently into the phone. He turned to me, sound returned to my ears.

"Dad, I think that's him! He looks just like him! If that's him, I had just auditioned for one of his plays at school!" I said, astonished that he could be in San Francisco.

I continued to walk toward him until I was standing just a few short feet in front of him. He had just disconnected his call. He looked slightly different than the instructor at Bowling Green. Perhaps, I was wrong and it was not him, after all.

I took a chance.

"Hi, is your name Mike Beak?" I asked.

"Hi," he replied in an unmistakable high-pitched voice. "Yes, it is. And, you are?"

As soon as he began to speak, I knew it was him.

He seemed to recognize my face; though, it appeared, he could not remember from where he knew me. His face held a look as though he was being solicited for a romantic date.

"My name is Christopher Price. I'm a student at Bowling Green. I auditioned for one of your plays a couple of weeks ago."

"Oh, yes, I remember you." He said, still looking at me as though I was trying to date him.

As he looked in the direction to where my daddy stood, I took the opportunity to introduce them to one another, "This is my father. Dad, this is Mike Beak. He's an instructor at Bowling Green," I said.

Mr. Beak's look changed. His demeanor became more professional. I wondered if initially he thought that my daddy and I were lovers or best friends, rather than father and son.

"How are you, Mr. Beak? I'm Andrew. My son says that you're an instructor in the theater department at B.G. I don't believe in coincidence; everything happens for a reason. With that being said, I believe we were supposed to meet you here. You may or may not know, but my son is graduating in the spring. He wants to move to L.A. to pursue acting, but I'd like for him to get a graduate degree. I believe it will make him more marketable as an actor. Do you know of any good acting schools around here?"

"Well, sure, I do," Mr. Beak began, "There are a lot of acting schools here: ACT, Berkeley has a good program, there are a lot of small theater schools, oh, and there's UC, Davis, they have a good program," Mr. Beak said.

"UC, Davis? This guy on the train mentioned that school," I said.

"Oh, it's a very good school. It's one of the better acting schools in the country, but if you're thinking of going there, you'd better hurry. Most of the schools have already chosen their graduate students for the fall term."

"Well, Mr. Beak, it really has been worthwhile running into you! What brings you to San Francisco?" My daddy asked.

"Oh, I love San Francisco! It's one of my favorite places in the world! I love the people, the culture, the diversity, the architecture; it's really just a fabulous city!" Mr. Beak said, endearingly.

"I have to say that I agree with you. From what my son and I have seen of it, it's a great place," my daddy concluded.

It truly was not in my plan to attend graduate school. As my daddy had expressed, my plan was to go directly to Los Angeles. However, there was something about the University of California in Davis that beckoned to me.

Something within me urged me to pursue enrolling at UC Davis. After my daddy and I had parted with Mr. Beak, we took the train back to the hotel. While my daddy rested, I went to the business center of the hotel to research the theater department at the University of California, Davis.

I loved the school at first sight. Like Bowling Green State University, UC Davis was located in a small city that encompassed the school. As were most cities in California, Davis was gorgeous. The campus was situated on acres upon acres of beautifully landscaped green grass with walking and biking trails strategically placed throughout the city. The theater and dance departments had recently merged and were operated by a newly appointed chairman. The newly formed department boasted of having an interdisciplinary theater program in which the students all learned from one another's discipline: that is, actors or directors may have had to learn the craft of set designers; dancers were possibly given acting roles; costume designers could have been assigned dancers' roles. It was a wonderful program.

I was totally impressed! Although acting had become my passion, I was very much interested in learning the manner in which the other students created within their crafts as well. As soon as I returned to our hotel room, I called the University.

"Hi, my name is Christopher Price. I am interested in enrolling in the university's theater program in acting," I said into the phone receiver.

"Well, hello, Christopher, I am Elizabeth Black, the graduate administrator here in the theater department at Davis. It's a pleasure to talk with you," Ms. Black said kindly. "In order to be admitted for the fall, you have to complete the department's application package and submit a video recording of yourself performing two monologues. But, Christopher, there is a deadline." She said in her soft voice. "Everything must be submitted by January 15th, that's a little less than three weeks away. Will you be able to meet the deadline?" Ms. Black asked softly.

"Yes, ma'am. I'm going to begin the process right now. Thank you for all of your help. You've been very kind," I said, sincerely.

"Oh, not a problem at all, Christopher! I look forward to receiving your documents and material."

"Okay. Thank you, Ms. Black."

"You are very welcome. And, please, call me Elizabeth. We do things differently in the theater department; we're not as stuffy as some of the other departments on campus," Elizabeth laughed, genuinely.

I laughed with her. "Okay, Elizabeth. I'll talk with you soon."

The following day, my daddy and I flew to Atlanta from San

Francisco. Once in Atlanta, I wasted no time getting into my car and driving home to Ohio. I had already told Malcolm about everything that transpired in San Francisco. He could not believe that my daddy and I had seen Mike Beak while we were in San Francisco. Malcolm was well-acquainted with Mr. Beak, as he had taken a class of his and he had also auditioned for some of Mr. Beak's theatrical productions.

I was on a mission: I had to become a student at the University of California, Davis. After my arrival in Bowling Green, I completed the application, wrote a personal statement, and I hand-delivered the forms to my instructors, so that they could complete letters of recommendations on my behalf. The next day, I rented a video camera from the technology department on campus. Malcolm and I went into one of the lecture halls and recorded me performing two monologues: *"Ain't I a Woman?"* by Sojourner Truth and a monologue from an August Wilson play *"Ma Rainey's Black Bottom."* We finished the pieces at three a.m., and not a moment too soon. I had to rush-deliver the package in order to meet the deadline of January 15th.

I felt accomplished. I knew that I would submit everything by the deadline, but it was work to doing so. I was particularly pleased with my monologues. The first piece by Sojourner Truth was actually a speech, of sorts, that she had given in the 1850s. Typically, actors did not perform roles that are written for the opposite sex. Gender bending, as it was called, occurred, of course, though rarely.

I was moved by Sojourner Truth's words and the tenacity that it took for her to present the speech about racism, religion, and sexism in a room filled with Whites before slavery had even been abolished. The courage it took for her to speak the truth astounded me. I had to perform the piece! I felt like I needed to share Ms. Truth's experiences as a tribute to all women: Black, Brown, and White.

The second piece I performed was equally compelling. It was written by the late, African American playwright, August Wilson. In the monologue, one of the central characters, Levee, detailed his experience with racism. He began by relating the rape of his mother by a mob of White men and ended the story by sharing the account of his father's death at the hands of racist Whites.

The piece was incredibly emotional and thought-provoking; in that, it not only told of a man's experience with racism, but it also showed how little one can truly know about a person by simply judging him according to his exterior.

~~~

Our spring break was rapidly approaching at Bowling Green. Malcolm and his best friend, Jackson, had planned an excursion to South Beach, Florida. He extended an invitation to me to join them, which I quickly accepted. Originally, I had planned to have my own hotel room, but, having made last minute plans to go, I found that all of the coastal hotels were booked. Malcolm offered to allow me to stay in the room with Jackson and him. I was hesitant at first to accept his offer. I did not want to encroach upon their time in the beautiful city. Malcolm and I were not technically in a relationship. My presence there may have interfered with their plans as single persons. Yet, at Malcolm's urging, I acquiesced.

I had come to the conclusion that Florida was simply an extraordinarily beautiful state. I had now visited the state two times and, on both occasions, I was equally impressed. Aside from

California, it was the closest to paradise that I had ever experienced.

Malcolm and Jackson arrived in Miami before me. Once I arrived, I took a shuttle to the hotel where we were staying. It was not as close to the beach as the one where my cousins and I had stayed, but it was nicer and more spacious.

We were excited to see each other. It felt strange seeing Malcolm and Jackson out of our usual environments: Bowling Green or Detroit. Yet, despite our happiness at seeing one another, Malcolm and I started bickering almost immediately. Irritated by the quarrels, I told Jackson and him to explore the city without me. Malcolm tried to get me to go along with them, but I was being stubborn and stayed behind.

After a couple of hours of being in the hotel room, I decide to put an end to my own personal pity party. I showered and put on a pair of gym shorts that I had bought through an online clothier. The shorts were extremely tight and far too short. They were made in the fashion of the jersey pants that football players wore. I ordinarily did not wear things that were so provocative, but, just like the time before when I visited Florida, I intended to be as uninhibited as I could be while I was there.

As soon as I stepped outside of the hotel, people began to honk the horns of their cars at me. I was awe-struck. I could not believe the amount of attention I received; after all, I was in Florida, from what I had gauged, people walked around nearly nude all the time. I felt uncomfortable. Contrary to my garb, I did not like to have direct attention drawn to me. I thought about going back to the hotel to put on a shirt, at least; however, I steeled myself, and grabbed a pair of sunglasses from my book bag, foolishly thinking that they would offer me some form of anonymity.

After I strolled along the beach for an hour or so, I began the journey back to the hotel room. When I arrived there, Malcolm and Jackson were gone. I showered and got into bed. Hours later, during the wee hours of morning, someone began banging on the door. I got up from the bed and looked through the peep hole to see Malcolm and Jackson standing on the other side.

"I forgot my key!" Malcolm said as soon as I opened the door.

"Oh," I responded as I got back into bed, swiftly drifting back into deep sleep.

"Girl, there was so many people there!" Jackson exclaimed to Malcolm.

"I know, right?! Girl, that line was out the door!" Malcolm said, giggling.

The sound of their voices roused me. I teetered between consciousness and sleep, until...

"Girl, I can't believe y'all was kissing on the dance floor and he pulled yo' dick out!"

A dead silence descended onto the room. I stopped breathing. My spine stiffened; yet, contrary to my inner feelings, a faint smile covered face. Slowly, I began to breathe again. I drifted back to sleep.

～～～

"So, you were on the dance floor slopping slob with some nigga, huh?" I asked the following afternoon, soon after we had all risen from bed.

"What?" Malcolm smiled innocently. It was an unintentional reaction of his to smile when he felt cornered.

"You heard me. You down here kissing some nigga that you don't even know!"

"We ain't together!" Malcolm exclaimed.

"So what! That makes it cool for you to be kissing on somebody you just met?! That's some nasty ass shit!"

"We wasn't doin' nothing, but kissin'!" Malcolm said emphatically.

"Nothing, but kissing?! You don't know where that nigga's mouth been! That's what I'm saying about you, you ain't got no damn standard! And, you talking all this shit about being so in-love! You got a lot to learn about love."

"Well, you act like you don't want me! I'm gone live my life!"

"So, yo' idea of living yo' life is kissing a nigga that you don't know, ain't never seen before, and ain't gone never see again?! Then, you let him pull out yo' dick on the dance floor?! That's trifling! I'm done with this shit before it even get started!" I said, in reference to our courtship.

"Fine." Malcolm said nonchalantly.

Malcolm and I successfully avoided one another for the remainder of the day. Later, during the evening, as he and Jackson dressed for the evening, Malcolm asked me if I would go to the club with them. I declined obstinately. I did not want to see his face or to hear his voice. I was hurt and disappointed by his actions.

Early the following morning, Malcolm and Jackson returned to the room. They engaged in their usual chit-chat before going to sleep. Malcolm and I slept together; although, we made certain that we did not touch one another during the night.

I slept soundly throughout the night. After I packed my things, I hugged Jackson and told him how great it was seeing him.

I looked at Malcolm, "I'll see you," I said as I walked from the room.

As I sat in the airport terminal awaiting my flight, I felt like the weight of the world rested on my chest. I shook my head in doubt and confusion. My stomach began to feel queasy. Something was wrong.

"No, no, no," I said to myself.

This cannot be happening. I looked around at the people in the terminal. I felt like the world was closing-in around me. I placed my face in my hands to gain an understanding of what was going on; what I was feeling. I do not know how it happened or even when it happened, but the budding of love began to blossom within me.

I looked down at my cell phone. I wanted to speak to him. I needed to speak to him. But what would I say? That I loved him? That I wanted him to be in my life? I was unsure, so I allowed my heart to foolishly dictate my actions and relinquished my rational thoughts in favor of my feelings.

"A, what's up?" I said into the receiver of my cell phone.

"Hi," his deep voice resonated through the phone. I could tell that he was smiling.

"I miss you."

"I miss you, too." Malcolm replied transparently.

"I, uh, I love you." I said hesitantly.

I could tell that he was smiling, again. "I love you, too, but where that come from? I thought you didn't want to see me again," Malcolm said softly.

"I didn't. At least, I thought I didn't, but I can't help or deny what I feel."

"So, what does that mean?" He asked.

"I don't know. Let's just play it by ear and see where it leads us."

~~~

"Hi, Christopher. How are you?" Elizabeth greeted.

"Hi, Elizabeth! I'm well. How are you?" I asked.

"I'm great, Christopher! Well, without further ado, on behalf of the faculty members and staff here at Davis, I'd like to extend an offer for you to join us for an interview with our graduate department. Will you accept?" Elizabeth asked.

"Well, yes!" I laughed, graciously.

Elizabeth whispered into the phone conspiratorially. "This is a big deal, Christopher. Your chances of being accepted into the University look very promising!"

My smile widened across my face. "Thank you, Elizabeth!"

I had to hurry to pack. I had just arrived back in Toledo from Florida when the phone call had come in from Elizabeth. I had to be in California in two days. Although the University would pay for my stay at a local bed and breakfast for one day, it was my responsibility to pay for any days that I chose to stay beyond the first day.

Elizabeth encouraged me to fly into Sacramento where they would send a shuttle-bus to get me, as opposed to flying into San Francisco where no transportation would be provided, because of the distance from the school.

I was ecstatic; yet, I had very little money for a flight to Sacramento. I had depleted the majority of my funds while I was in Florida. However, after calling my daddy to tell him of my good news, he not only expressed his joy of my accomplishment, but he also called his friend who was able to get me a standby ticket through the airline where she worked. I was thrilled. My dreams were coming together perfectly.

~~~

Tribulations rarely took breaks in my life. Oftentimes they were intertwined with my blessings; no matter what was going on in my life, tragedy always seemed to find a way of entering my life, making the act of living difficult.

"Chris, did you hear about Aunt Carol?" Autumn asked sobbing.

My heart had skipped a beat, pitter-patted, then began to beat at a heightened pace.

"No, what happened?" I asked through my grief-stricken throat, preparing myself for the worst.

"They said her cancer ain't getting better. She was forced to quit work, 'cause there ain't nothing else they can do for her," Autumn said through tears, grasping for air in between her labored sobs.

It saddened me that she was forced to experience grief at such a young age. Aunt Carol was special to her, far more than simply a great-aunt.

"We'll be okay, Autumn. We just have to enjoy every day that we have with her," I said soothingly.

~~~

Although Sacramento was the capital of California, its airport was not nearly as big or as spectacular as the San Francisco Airport, nor was the city as breathtaking as the Bay Area. I was taken aback by its plain-looking facade. I assumed every city in California looked like San Francisco.

Though, no picturesque hills adorned the landscape of Sacramento; no charming trolley cars occupied the streets; no tall sky scrapers stretched to the heavens. The city was somewhat drab; it reminded me of Toledo.

I quietly absorbed the scenery through the window of the shuttle, while visions of what lay ahead of me twirled throughout my mind.

"This is where you will be staying, sir." The driver of the shuttle-bus said as he parked in front of a splendid cottage home.

"Thank you," I smiled, handing him a token of my appreciation for his gracious service.

Across the street from the Bed and Breakfast sat a glimpse of the University's campus. It was purely exquisite. I longed to walk through the paths nestled between the lush, green grass.

I hurriedly took my luggage into the Inn. After checking-in, Jane, the hostess, escorted me to the room that I would occupy. We passed several bedrooms along the way to mine. Jane explained that each room was named for its uniqueness in décor. My room was spacious and airy. The well-polished hardwood floors suited the Victorian-styled furniture well.

"Oh, wow! That bed looks so comfortable!" I said as I eyed the plush queen-sized bed.

"Our guests speak very highly of the bed. Many of them say that they don't want to return home to their own beds after sleeping in ours," Jane smiled proudly.

After Jane left me to attend to her duties, I looked around the room. It was really beautiful and well-maintained. The adjoining bathroom was clean and nicely decorated as well. I sat down in an accent chair for only a moment before I walked downstairs and, then, outside. I wanted to view the campus before my upcoming interview in a couple of hours.

Just as the photos depicted, the grounds of the campus were immaculate. I walked around for an hour before I rushed back to the

Bed and Breakfast to shower and to change for the interview with the faculty members.

~~~

"Hey, Dad. I made it to California," I said into my cellphone.

"Okay, good, son. How is it, so far?" My daddy asked.

"It's nice. I walked around the campus. It's beautiful…Uhm, have you heard about Aunt Carol?" I asked sorrowfully.

"Yeah, I spoke with Carol earlier today…I'll finally be running things. I'm getting Felicia's ass out of there!" He said excitedly.

Felicia had continued to care for Mother since I had moved to Bowling Green. Aunt Carol supported Felicia's assistance of Mother, though, because of my daddy's animosity toward Felicia, he did not want her to care for Mother.

"Uh, okay…I'm going to get ready for my interview with the administrators," I said, ending the call.

I did not know if he was serious about putting Felicia out of Mother's house, though, even if he was not, I would have thought that Aunt Carol's health would have taken precedence above anything else, not his presumed rise to power.

~~~

"Hi, Christopher. I'm Aaron Biederman. I am the acting chair of the Theatre and Dance Department." Mr. Biederman said in a smooth voiced, laced with an English accent. Aaron was a tall, attractive gentleman of about sixty years of age. He bore a strong resemblance to the Irish actor Liam Neeson.

"It's a pleasure to meet you, Mr. Biederman." I said as I accepted his outstretched hand.

"Please call me, Aaron. Yes?" He asked. I nodded my head affirmatively. "And, this is my wife, Rachel. She is also an instructor here at Davis." I shook her hand and all of the other twelve instructors and staff members that were gathered for the interview.

"Christopher, we all here had an opportunity to view the video tape as well as the other documents that, uh, you sent us, and we must say that we are very pleased with what we saw," Aaron complimented.

"Thank you, Aaron."

"Now, Christopher, how long have you been acting?"

"I just started about nine months ago," I said easily.

"Well, you are very talented. As you must know, most of the students here have been acting for most of their lives."

"Thank you. Well, I kind of figured that they had; that is the case with the students at the school where I am currently a student as well."

The fact that I had never been trained as an actor was an issue of contention for some of my peers. They felt that my skill should have been indicative of long years of training.

"Have you ever been in any productions?" Aaron asked.

I began to feel slightly uneasy. I wondered if they had invited me all the way there just to tell me that I lacked enough experience to attend the school.

"I've been in only one production. It was a play entitled, 'Quiet in the Land'. It was based on the Amish experience in Ontario, Canada during the early 1900s."

"You were cast in an Amish play?" Aaron asked interestingly.

"Yes," I said naively.

His interest sparked my curiosity. I had never thought about the fact that as a Black man I was playing an Amish character.

"Well, Christopher, I suppose that means that others recognize your talent as well." He and the other faculty members and staff laughed good-naturedly.

I smiled shyly. I appreciated his compliment, but I felt uncomfortable receiving it. I was not yet used to people applauding a talent in which I was yet aware.

"Thank you," I replied humbly.

"Christopher, we'd like to open our doors here to you as a graduate student. Do you accept our invitation?" Aaron asked, smiling.

"Yes!" I said returning his smile.

I shook hands with all of the assembled persons, thanking each of them. Afterwards, Elizabeth ushered me into the graduate office to tell me that I would hear from the department within a week to go over my award package. I gave her a big, warm hug and thanked her for her hospitality.

I stayed in Davis until the following day. Somehow Elizabeth had arranged for the shuttle to take me to the San Francisco airport. My daddy felt that I would have had a greater chance of getting a flight back home from San Francisco than from Sacramento. Although standby or buddy passes were convenient as a last minute resort, particularly when trying to avoided exorbitant airline fees, they were not always practical.

I arrived at the San Francisco airport shortly after one o'clock p.m. My flight was scheduled to depart at three p.m., however, when I arrived at the boarding gate, the agent informed that the flight was overbooked. I had to wait until the next flight, which was scheduled to leave at five thirty p.m.

Five-thirty had come and gone. Like the airplane before it, the plane was filled to capacity. My daddy called his airline friend to see if there was another flight that I could take that would get me closer to Ohio, though there was none. Students across the country were going or coming from their schools' spring break. Flights were completely booked.

I sat at the airport for another fourteen hours. I had to get home. Our final exams were that week. *Had I made a mistake by going to Davis?* I could not miss my finals. There would be no opportunity for me to re-take them. If I did not take the exams, I would fail the semester, which would inevitably mean that I would not graduate.

I had no other choice:

"Dad, can you buy me an airline ticket, and I'll pay you back when I get home?" I said into the phone's receiver.

I absolutely dreaded asking my daddy for money. I did not like to ask much of anything from anyone, but I really deplored asking him; he always overly-dramatized the event. I had promised myself while I was incarcerated that I would never ask him for any money for as long as I lived. I had done well so far, but circumstances had a way of making me into a liar.

"Chris, do you know how much the tickets are?" He asked.

"Yes, they're running around $590 for a one way ticket to Detroit."

"Six hundred dollars for a one-way ticket?!"

"Yea, it's spring break and a last minute ticket."

"And, you're going to pay me back when you get to Toledo?" He asked insistently.

"Yes," I replied.

Before I called my daddy, I had called my uncle and cousin to ask them if I could borrow the money to give back to my daddy for the airline ticket. My uncle was my grandfather's brother and very reliable; my cousin had his own business as a labor contractor and was doing well for himself, so I knew that I could depend on them for the loan. They both said that I could pay them back in increments. I had much rather owed them, than to be in debt with my daddy.

"Okay. I'll call you when it's been taken care of."

"All right. Thank you." I said as I disconnected the call.

HE TOLD ME

~~~

I arrived home with little time to prepare for my exams, but I was grateful just to be home to take them. After I had reviewed the material to study for the finals, I called my cousin to arrange a time when I could come to get the money to pay my daddy.

"A, De-De, what's up?"

"A, dude, what's up?"

"Not too much. I was calling to see if I can come get the money you said I can borrow?"

"Oh, oh. Naw, dude. I ain't got it," he replied.

"Huh? I thought you said you had it."

"Naaaw, I ain't even got it," he said.

I thought for a moment before I conceded, "All right."

I did not want to go back and forth with him about the money. If he said that he did not have it, there was nothing that I could do but to accept what he said. The only issue lied in how was I going to pay back my daddy?

"Dad, I don't have the money that I borrowed from you for my airline ticket," I said into the phone.

"What do you mean?" He asked.

"I asked De-De and Uncle Sam if I could borrow the money for the plane ticket and they both told me that I could, but, when I just spoke to De-De, he said that he didn't have the money."

"So, how are you going to get the money to pay me back?" He inquired.

"I don't know. I'm going to figure out something."

"Yea, all right," he replied irritatingly.

I could not believe the dilemma that I had inadvertently created for myself. I did not think that De-De would deceive me. I had no one else that I could turn to for the money to pay my daddy. My plan was to pay Uncle Sam and De-De back in fifty dollar increments until I had paid them both three hundred dollars, which collectively amounted to the money that I owed my daddy. I did not know what to do. Yet, as life would have it, things were to get worse.

"Where my money?" The words erupted from his mouth the moment I answered the phone. No hello; simply the abrasive inquiry.

I did not have time to remind myself that it was my daddy on the other end of the phone line.

"What?!" I asked angrily. I felt the brows of my eyes knit; my face constricted in anger.

"Where my money?!" He repeated harshly.

I did not like anyone speaking to me in a disrespectful manner. I tried my best to address everyone that I encountered with the dignity and respect entitled to every human being. I understood that I owed my daddy money and that, from his vantage, it may have appeared that I had taken advantage of him, but there was a better way that he could have spoken to me, rather than as though he was talking to a stranger on the street.

"I ain't got it!" I said coldly in an even tone into the phone.

"When I'ma get my money?!" He asked again in the same pseudo-threatening tone.

I did not know with whom he had been talking to give him the thug-sensation from which he was operating, but it did little for me. Very little in life frightened me. I could not be intimidated, whether by my daddy who, in his mind, had miraculously transformed himself into a thug or by a real-life gangsta'.

"You gone get yo' money when I give it to you!" I replied sinisterly.

"Yeah, all right," he conceded before abruptly terminating the phone call.

I did not like to behave in the way that I had, especially toward my father; however, I was not going to allow him to call me and to speak to me in a condescending tone as though I was the scum of the earth. It was not going to happen.

~~~

I got the call. I was accepted to the University of California, Davis. The Spirit of God had truly intervened on my behalf. I was not only going to attend one of the best theater programs in the country, but I was also given a full scholarship and paid positions as an instructor and a research assistant during three of the semesters.

Ironically, considering the drastic turn in our relationship, a trip that began as a simple excursion to San Francisco with my father had begun to forge the way for my future. California, here I come!

Chapter Fourteen

The candescent moon spilled into the room. The glow of the light illuminated his dark skin creating an eerie-looking silhouette of his body. He heaved in and out deeply, passionately. The sound of his voice filled my ears. 'Yes! Yesss! Yeeesss!' He groaned in ecstasy. I was aroused; yet, angered by his moans of pleasure. He moved onto his back, throwing his long, thin legs up and then behind him. They dangled limply as if they were held from the ceiling by strings. I began to sweat profusely. My role as voyeur was far more than I could handle emotionally and mentally.

A shift in the lighting made it possible for me to catch a small glimpse of the perpetrator. I moved my head from right to left; straining my neck to see the face of the violator, though to no avail. His long hair and the darkened room made it impossible for me to see him clearly. He leaned over, caressing Malcolm's inner thighs with his tongue; seductively licking his abdomen until Malcolm squirmed. My blood pressure rose; my head throbbed as I watched him move his open mouth to Malcolm's throbbing, erect penis. His long flowing dreads parted. He looked up. Our eyes locked onto one another's.

What?! Him?! Not him, of all the people in the world, it could not be him! Rage consumed me. I raced toward my betrayer with outstretched arms. Grabbing his neck, I squeezed tightly. He gazed into my eyes, a smile spread across his face. I released my stronghold, falling to the floor as I sobbed in anguish.

My eyes flung open. I breathed laboriously. I sat upright in the bed, looking around the room. Malcolm slept peacefully beside me, unaware of the terror that I had just consumed me. I touched his back, pulling him toward me as I laid back down beside him, until I had drifted into a slumber.

The following morning, with the events of the dream fresh in my mind, I questioned him.

"Mally," I called him by the nickname that I had given him. "Are you attracted to Tommie?"

He smiled sweetly. My question had caught him off guard. His smile was confirmation that there was some degree of truth to the dream.

"I guess," he smiled uneasily.

Tommie was a good friend of mine who I had allowed to live with me. He had been sleeping in the second bedroom of my apartment for a couple of weeks. Yet, over the past week, I had begun to feel an energy developing between Mally and him. It was innocent in the beginning, just a common interest in the other. However, it soon became more: a prolonged look in each other's eyes; a sharing of intimate, personal space; an inquiry of one another's whereabouts.

"And, you're cool with that? You don't have an issue with being attracted to my friend?"

"No," he chuckled nervously. "What am I supposed to do? You can't help who you attracted to," he replied matter-of-factly.

"No, a person can't help with whom he is attracted, but he can take measures to prevent or control the attraction. I would have never allowed myself to like or be attracted to Jackson or any of your friends. I would have kept my conversations with them to a minimum, if I felt that I was becoming attracted to them."

He thought deeply before he responded.

"Well, it's your fault that I have these feelings for him!" He accused.

"Feelings?! Oh, you have feelings for him?!" I asked astonishingly.

"I don't know."

I snickered. "And, how in the hell is it my fault?" I asked incredulously.

"Because you brought him around; you let him stay here," he replied.

I felt that I was watching a crazy episode of *The Maury Povich Show*. I was not, however. Strangely, my life had come to parallel the topics of outlandish talk-shows.

In my spirit, I knew that something like what we were experiencing would occur. Although Mally and I had many things in common, we had very different values. I esteemed the act of love-making and the sanctity of it; however, Mally thought little of the intimacy of sex. To him, having sex was nearly equivalent to holding hands. The act of sharing his intimate sexual parts with someone was not a big deal to Mally.

"Are you saying that I cannot trust you with my friends; that every time I bring someone around you, I have to wonder if you gone be attracted to him?" I asked.

"Well, naw…"

"That's what it sounds like you're saying to me! So, what is your hope? Do you want to have sex with him or something?"

"I would 'have' with him." He said nonchalantly, indicating that he would have sex with him.

I could not have said with absolute certainty that I would not have had a similar experience, if I had dated or fallen in-love with someone older than Mally, but I believed that the likelihood of such an occurrence diminished with age; or, at least, I hoped so.

~~~

"Little Chris?" My cousin, Felicia, said into the phone.

"Hey there, bae." I responded.

"How you doin'?" She asked.

"I'm all right. Trying to knock out this term paper, but I don't feel like writing   it."

"Oh, yea, I remember those days. Mmmhmm…well, just stick with it. Have you spoken to your father?"

"Uhn uh, no, I haven't."

"Well, I think he may have fired you." Felicia expressed somberly.

"Huh?" I asked.

"Well, he came over here the other day with John Henry

and was telling him what cleaning he needed done around the house."

I instinctively laughed aloud. My daddy was incredibly immature and vindictive. We had not spoken to one another since our phone conversation regarding the money that I owed him. His way of getting back at me was by supposedly firing me from a position in which he had not given me.

Shortly after I had permanently moved to Bowling Green for school, I applied for a job at Wendy's to help to cover the cost of my living expenses. After a few short days of applying for the job, I was hired as a grill cook. Though, because I was in B.G., on most days, Mother had no one to clean her home or to give Felicia a break from her duties as Mother's primary care giver. Aunt Carol asked me if I would quit my job at Wendy's to continue caring for Mother on a part-time basis and that she would compensate me for doing so. I accepted her request: it would allow me to see Mother more often, and I would still be able to pay my monthly expenses.

Though, as my daddy had stated, with Aunt Carol being terminally ill, things would be changing, since he was now in control of Mother's affairs. *Not everyone should be given power.* Sadly, in his attempt to affect me, he was actually hurting his mother, for it was she who needed my care of her. However, Mother's need was not a concern of his; at least, not as much as getting revenge against his son.

"He is something else. Okay. Thank you for calling me, but I'll be okay. I'm leaving for California soon," I said in appreciation of her phone call.

I soon learned that my daddy had also removed my name from his wholesale club membership. I used the membership to get household items for Mother's home. I was disappointed that he would go to the lengths that he did to hurt me, but I was not surprised. I had seen how he had gone out of his way to hurt those whom he supposedly loved. Despite having been "fired," I continued to go to Mother's to clean and care for her until I left for California.

~~~

The day had come. For the second time in my life, I was graduating from college. I had expected to feel differently; excited or elated. However, I did not. It was like any other ordinary day. My new focus was moving to California, completing my Master's degree, and becoming a successful actor. Having set other goals, diminished the joy of having already fulfilled one.

I was given four tickets to the ceremony. I extended invitations to my parents: Mymomme, my daddy and Sara. I had not expected my daddy to attend it, but I felt that I should still let him know that he was welcome to join me in my achievement. Although, he did not personally deny my invitation, Sara called to tell me that they would not be present.

Instead, Mymomme, Mama, Allen, and Brandy attended the ceremony with me. Interestingly, despite my nonchalance toward graduating, I really enjoyed having them present at the gala. In fact, their presence meant more to me than did achieving the degree. Their attendance at the event was an obvious indication of their support of me, despite my indifference toward the achievement.

Although, I was overjoyed by each of their presence at the graduation, I was especially pleased to see my grandfather. In the past, Allen had not attended such events. Though, as Allen aged, he had become very supportive of his family. Because of Allen, Mama, Mymomme, and Brandy, the day was far more than I had hoped or planned for it to be.

~~~

It was over. My relationship with Mally had come to an abrupt halt. Mally's attraction to Tommie proved to be more than the relationship could withstand, or more than I was willing to accept. We had been arguing over trivial matters ever since his disclosure regarding Tommie. In a final showdown, I angrily told him to leave my apartment. He packed his possessions and was gone by three o'clock the following morning.

Although I had initiated the severance of our relationship, I was devastated. I had fallen deeply in love with Mally. He was far more to me than simply a lover. We were friends. Our days had become consumed with time together: going to the movies, eating take-out Chinese food, watching episodes of "Sex in the City" on DVD, talking into the wee hours of the morning, and making passionate love. During the short time that we had known each other, he had become a permanent fixture in my soul.

With my relationship with Mally having ended, I felt an urgency to leave Ohio. Like so many others before me, I looked forward to the promise of California—the land of dreams. I not only wanted to fulfill my dreams of achieving a graduate degree and becoming a world-renowned actor, but I also wanted to put some distance between my family and me and all that I had gone through since I had been released from prison. Three thousand miles of distance was just what I felt that I needed to fully heal, rather than simply going with the flow of things until something else catastrophic occurred.

Chapter Fifteen

The blazing sun greeted me the moment I exited the airplane in Los Angeles. I raced to the baggage claim area to retrieve my luggage. I called my friend, Erin, to let him know that I had arrived in Los Angeles. After I told him of my acceptance to U.C. Davis, he had decided to move to California as well.

"Hey, chile!!!" He greeted into the phone.

I laughed at his enthusiastic salutation. I needed his jovial spirit. Although California was where I wanted to be, I missed Mally. He and I had visited with one another the day before I left for California and mended our broken hearts. We tried as best we could to bandage our severed relationship; yet, we were a day too late.

"Hey there! I just got my stuff from baggage claim. I'll wait for you at the train depot," I said exuberantly into the cellphone.

"Okay, chile! Honey, I can't wait to see my soror!" Erin shouted into the phone, making use of the sorority jargon that he had learned while he was a student at Central State University.

I laughed. "Okay, I'll see you soon."

Two hours had passed before Erin finally arrived. He explained that he was distracted by a cute boy on the way to get me. *Typical, Erin.* I laughed away the irritation I felt for having to wait so long for him. As we drove to my cousin's house where I would be staying, we talked about all that had been going on during the week that he had been in Los Angeles.

"Girl, I mean, chile, I'm lovin' L.A.! This city is cute! I been all up and through Hollywood, chile!" He said excitedly.

"Where are you staying?"

"Chile, I'm staying in Inglewood, honey! But, girl, I mean, chile, I got to get me a job and find somewhere else to live. Honey, I met the guy I'm staying with online and he trippin' already. But chile, it ain't nothin' but a chicken wing, honey! I'll find me somewhere else! A bitch know how to survive, honey!" He exclaimed as he cocked his head to the side and pursed his lips.

He was hilarious. After about an hour of battling Los Angeles' infamous traffic, we arrived at Diane's house in Long Beach.

Diane and my mother were first cousins and one year apart in age. I had not seen her since I was very young child; so young that I did not remember meeting her. I only recalled the photos that Mama had of Diane and her younger sisters; however, the moment that she opened her front door, I felt as though she had been with me every day of my life.

"Chris?" She said as she unlocked the steel security door.

"Hi, Diane!" I greeted, giving her a firm hug. "This is my childhood friend, Erin," I introduced.

I loved Diane from the moment I stepped one foot into her home. I was beyond grateful that she allowed me to stay with her. As an ex-felon, I understood how people negatively viewed us, regardless of whether we were related to them or not. She did not know me and, yet, she had welcomed me into her home with an open heart and outstretched arms.

Generally expressing, Los Angeles was a gorgeous city; however, it was not what I expected it to be from watching television and movies, but it did have its own unique beauty. For starters, contrary to the depiction of Hollywood on the Big Screen, the real Hollywood was only several blocks long. It was not nearly as impressive as it was portrayed.

My plan was to only be in Southern California for a short period of time before school began in the fall. While there in L.A., it was my hope to become familiar with the world of film acting, as my training had been in theater. I busied myself by disseminating my photos and resume to several acting agencies; yet, no one called me.

Booger and Tookie's aunt, Annie, lived and worked in L.A., as an actress for years. She showed me around the city and gave me a lot of information on the acting industry there. She encouraged me to apply to one of the casting agencies as an Extra to get my name and face known throughout the city. Extras performed a variety of roles on television and film. They were the actors seen in non-speaking roles; however, some Extras were given speaking parts as well, for which they were compensated.

My mentor and former instructor from Bowling Green, Amy Ainsworth, strongly advised me not to appear as an Extra too often. She did not want me to be viewed as simply an Extra, but as a legitimate talent, whose talent should be taken seriously and not as just another body to fill the television or movie screen.

After applying to the city's largest casting agent, I immediately began getting calls to work as an Extra in many of the most popular shows on television. Though, in heeding Amy's advice, I only accepted assignments for the most popular shows that may have led to speaking roles on other shows.

~~~

Mally and I had remained in communication with one another after my move to California. During the first days of my stay in California everything between us seemed great, however, by the second week, things began to go awry. Hours elapsed without a single phone call from Mally. When he finally called, he was very indifferent regarding his absence and lack of communication. I felt that, in order for our relationship to work, we needed to maintain effective, consistent communication with one another. My words fell on deaf ears. Mally had no interest in what I said.

With distance between us, Mally had become more fully aware of a great truth: I was deeply in love with him. According to his understanding, the depth of my love rendered me vulnerable; I no longer had the advantage or power, as he perceived it, that I had once wielded in the relationship. He was correct: the depth of my love for him had made me emotionally vulnerable and impotent.

Over the next several weeks, our relationship was a merry-go-round of break-ups and make-ups, until finally it seemed that the relationship had truly met its demise.

I, however, was unwilling to accept the inevitable. Distraught and brokenheartedly, I flew to Ohio to be with Mally before my school term began.

Mally was unaware that I was had flown to Bowling Green, and, while we had only been estranged for one week, he had already moved on and found a new beau. Although Mally maintained that they had not consummated their attraction for one another, the tell-tale signs of their sexual intimacy were apparent on Mally's face in the form of small, white bumps that surrounded his lips and covered his chin—Mally had contracted a sexually transmitted infection.

Yet, despite the obvious ramifications of his sexual escapades, I was not deterred. Foolishly, days after the infection had healed, we made love ardently. I remained in Bowling Green with Mally until it was time for me to return to California to begin school. Upon my departure, Mally and I vowed to make our relationship work, despite the great distance that separated us.

Chapter Sixteen

The first few weeks of my life in Davis, California were filled with mixed emotions. Achieving a graduate degree was a bit different than achieving an undergraduate degree. Graduate classes were much longer and far more boring than undergraduate courses. My instructors spent huge amounts of time discussing topics of little significance. In one particular class, we conversed for three hours about the various components of space and what those varied interpretations meant to us. The topic of discussion was hardly worthy of a three minute discourse, let alone three hours.

I sat through hour after hour of the courses in agony. My only joy and reprieve presented itself in the course that I instructed. On Tuesdays and Thursday of each morning, I taught an introductory acting class. My class consisted largely of students who took the course I instructed as an elective. I promised myself that I would show the students the joys of acting and the beauty of storytelling. I concluded that, they may not want to pursue acting as a career, though, by the time the course ended, they would have an appreciation for the craft of acting.

Aside from teaching, I found refuge in decorating my apartment. I spent large sums of my work-pay and monies from my student loans to furnish my home to my satisfaction. After leaving school for the day, I would rush home to utilize the computers in the apartment complex's business center to order furniture to fill the rooms of my apartment.

I chose to decorate the living and dining room in earth tones. I found a pretty, micro-fibered, crème-colored sofa and two brown accent chairs that looked beautiful in the small living area; and a round glass dining table with a large metal, tarnish-brown, base with four brown microfiber chairs. I went to a fabric store and created drapes for the living and dining room windows from a rustic, burnt-orange satin material. I used the same material to create throw pillows and a table cloth for the dining room table to better tie together the rooms.

On weekends, I would invite my classmates to my home for dinner. I would prepare a meal of baked chicken and gravy, homemade mashed potatoes, green beans, dinner rolls, and a chocolate cake for dessert. As was the case with my classmates in Bowling Green, many of my classmates at Davis seldom had home-cooked meals, because they attended school so far away from home. Yet, an act openly appreciated act of altruism by my classmates in Bowling Green was met with envy by my classmates in Davis.

Although my classmates in Davis expressed appreciation for the meal I prepared, many of them openly wondered how I, a struggling college student like them, could afford to decorate my home in the way that I had and to spend money on "lavish" dinners to feed them. They wondered how much I was being paid to teach and how much assistance I was receiving in scholarship monies.

Initially, I was dismayed that a simple act of kindness could garner so much contention; however, soon thereafter, I recalled Mother telling me a story when she had experienced similar sentiments from the ladies at her church during the 1950s. Again, Mother's words echoed through my mind as though she was sitting right beside me:

"I don't drink…I don't smoke…And, I don't gamble! I ought to have the things in life I want!"

With Mother's declaration fixed strongly in my mind, I released myself from any and all hurt feelings that I may have felt from my classmates actions.

~~~

The University of California in Davis was well-regarded as a great institution of learning; however, like Bowling Green, the city consisted primarily of White students. I had no issue with learning alongside White students; yet, oftentimes I felt alienated and alone, as though I was invisible. The vast majority of the students walked pass me without a kind look, a single word of greeting, or even a glance in my direction.

I spent hours in the gym filling the void I felt. Though, no amount of exercise quite filled my need for human companionship. I had managed to forge an acquaintanceship with one of my classmates. She was a great girl who had transferred to the States from Canada. She was kind and very intelligent; however, because of her own responsibilities as a student and instructor, we rarely had to time to get together to enjoy our lives outside of school.

Mally and I made another attempt at a long distance relationship. We resumed talking on the phone many times throughout each day; however, the distance proved to be too great for him. He needed the comfort of having me with him to share in his everyday experiences. I understood his need, but I felt that we could overcome the distance with phone calls and regular visits to see one another throughout the year; though, in the end, the previous turmoil in the relationship and the distance between us were too great, our relationship had finally met its end. The grief of my failed relationship and the abyss of loneliness threatened to consume me. I secretly yearned for someone with whom I could share my days.

~~~

Markese and I had met on a gay chat site in Bowling Green prior to my relationship with Mally. We had a short-lived sexual relationship for a couple of months until our strong personalities collided with one another.

Markese and I had not communicated for months after our parting, until shortly before I moved to California. I told him of my plans to attend graduate school in Davis and he informed me that he was moving to San Diego. We made a pact to remain in contact after our move to the sunshine state. Once I had moved into my apartment, I invited him to come to Davis for a few days as friends. He happily obliged.

Markese and I greeted one another with an old familiarity; yet anew. Markese had changed and grown since we had last seen each other. Having been raised in a middle-class suburb of Toledo, he was arrogant and pretentious. His association with Blacks, excluding his family members and his best friend, was very limited. As such, his view of us Blacks was narrow and restricted to what he saw on television and the local news stations. His slightly privileged upbringing had given him a demeanor of superiority.

However, the Markese that I greeted in Davis was far more subdued. He had always been incredibly intelligent, but now his intellect was coupled with maturity.

For many gays, bars and clubs were places where they could drink, be entertained, and to meet one another. Because I had never been much of a clubber, gay chat sites became my window and door into the gay community.

Our first introduction occurred on one of the more well-known chat sites. His photos depicted an older guy who was confident; sure of himself. His head rested against the back of what appeared to be a chair. His amber-colored eyes communicated maturity. I was interested in knowing more of the gentleman.

After our first few chats, he asked me to accompany him to a Christmas party. I declined, feeling that we did not know each other well enough to attend a formal gathering together. He graciously accepted my polite refusal. We maintained in contact with one another for days afterwards, until he asked if he could come to Davis to visit with me. I obliged.

I was in the business center of my apartment complex when he arrived. I saw him pull into a parking spot in a crème-colored Cadillac. The car suited him well; it was as classy and elegant as he had appeared in the photo.

I stood as I saw him approaching. He was very attractive. He looked more youthful in person than he had in the photo. He smiled as he saw me, exposing beautiful, straight teeth. He was dressed casually in a pair of jeans and a T-shirt.

I escorted him to my apartment where I introduced him to Markese. Wanting to be freshly dressed for our evening together, he asked if he could dress at my home, as the drive from Tracy, where he lived, was an about hour and a half from Davis. After he and Markese had exchanged pleasantries with one another, he and I went to my bedroom to dress for an evening at the theater, followed by dinner.

He emerged from the bathroom fully clothed. He looked wonderful: his dark, naturally wavy hair glistened under the light, the collar of his long-sleeved shirt stood at attention, creating an aura of regality beneath his well-shaved face. He was impeccably groomed from the hair on his head all the way down to his stylish, hard-soled shoes. Markese exited the second bedroom as we prepared to leave. He, too, was impressed with the guy's style and presentation.

The pleasantly, well-groomed stranger introduced himself as Charleston. As I watched him exit my apartment, I thought that his name fit him perfectly. He, like his name, exuded sophistication.

We arrived at a gate that led outside of the apartment complex. I opened the gate and moved aside for Charleston to pass through it, he placed his hand on the gate, insisting that I pass first. Initially, I thought that maybe he had an issue with a guy opening a door for him, but I dismissed the thought, thinking that my thought process was foolish. I smiled at him, encouraging him to pass through the gate. His features hardened; his eyes became fixed; his smile froze against the backdrop of his face. In one quick swoop, he placed his hand on the small of my back and firmly, though not so forceful as to shove, escorted me through the open gate.

By the time I was able to respond to his action, his face had returned to its pleasant appearance. I chronicled the action in my memory for future reference.

I was thoroughly displeased with the University's theater department. The primary reason that I had chosen to attend Davis' acting program rested on its curriculum. I wanted to further my knowledge of acting. Simply being blessed with a talent was not enough for me. I wanted to be able to have intellectual conversations about the discipline; I wanted to know who the major theorists and theories were of the art; and, as conveyed to me during my interview with the university, I wanted to learn more about the crafts of the other artists, i.e. set and costume designers, make-up artists, and directors.

If I was a visual artist, I would want to know the history of the works of such artists as Pablo Picasso and Leonardo da Vinci, rather than simply being exposed to what I was visually able to behold; if I was a singer, I would want to be familiar with the various registers and tonalities of the human voice, rather than only being able to sing a song; if I was a dancer, I would be interested in studying the innumerable forms of dance, rather than only knowing how to execute one style of dance. As a graduate student-actor, it was important to me to be well-educated in the art of acting as a whole.

In addition to my dissatisfaction with the program, many of my classmates had begun to act strangely toward me. I began to experience what I heard many Blacks express when working with Whites. While I could not be certain that my race was the reason as to their treatment of me, I was constantly aware of the fact that I was the only Black graduate student and the only Black in a position of authority as a student-instructor.

Being the only Black person in the graduate department made me feel even more alienated than I had in times past. To make matters worse, my classmates had somehow learned that I was personally chosen by Aaron Biederman to attend the university. I had begun to feel like I was Aaron's prodigy and the theater department's "token negro."

Soon afterwards, my talent as an actor became the topic of discussions. While faculty members and doctoral students praised my skill, my own classmates dissected my gift.

"I just feel like you always portray angry characters...did you rehearse your performance or was it kind of impromptu...how much training did you say you've had...how long have you been acting...how many performances have you been in..."

I had enough. I stopped attending my classes and I seldom went to any of the events that were required of graduate students. Eventually, I withdrew from the school. I was tired. I could have stayed at the university and demanded that their mistreatment toward me cease, but my nonchalance would not allow me. Instead, I left the institution with the hope of beginning a career as a professional actor.

~~~

With my matriculation at the University of California having come to an end, I was free to pursue my passion. I no longer had to sit through boring lectures about minuscule topics; I no longer had to suffer the ill-feelings of my classmates toward me; I no longer had to put my dreams on hold. The boundless skies were the limit. The only problem lay in, I had no plan. I had withdrawn from the university without a plan as to what I would do next. I had a dream to act, though no direction as to how I would achieve the endeavor.

And, to further compound my dilemma, the due date for my rent was quickly approaching and I did not have enough money saved to pay the expense.

For days, I sat in my apartment trying to decide what I would do next. Returning home to Ohio was not a thought even remotely worth considering. Moving to Los Angeles did not seem like a viable option as there were more opportunities in the Bay Area to act on stage than there were in L.A.

I was at a standstill. I had no place to go and my closest family members were over 300 miles away in Long Beach.

I paced through each room of my apartment over and over again trying to come to a decision as to what to do next. I had a thought, but then I quickly dismissed it from my mind. I began to pace, again. Yet, as I paced through the apartment several more times, the previously dismissed thought reemerged. It was the perfect solution to my quandary.

"Can I stay with you for a couple of weeks until I figure out my next move?" I asked uneasily. I understood that at times everyone needed someone, however, it was still unnerving for me to ask anything of anyone, especially someone whom I had only known for six months.

"Uh…," he stated hesitatingly.

A sixth sense chimed in my head; however, I misread what it meant.

"…if you don't want me to, it's cool. I understand." I said, interrupting his thought and preventing him from finishing his sentence.

"No, no, of course, you can stay. I'd love to have you."

Charleston said reassuringly.

"Okay…Thank you," I smiled. I thought for a brief moment as to the reason for his hesitation, yet, rather than to ask why he hesitated, I internally basked in the glory of his consent to allow me to live with him. Had I known better, I would have questioned him about the hesitancy—a mishap that would later cost me.

The following week, after I had packed my belongings and placed my furniture in storage, Charleston and I drove southeast of Davis for an hour and a half until we reached Charleston's home in Tracy, California.

I slept most of the way to the city. I could not help myself. The plush leather seats and smooth ride in Charleston's Cadillac Deville made sleeping hard to resist. We stepped out of the car into the heat of the ever-bright Californian sun. I stretched long and hard before I made the short trek to the front door.

As we stood on the small porch of the newly built, two-story home, Charleston placed his key in the lock and then turned to me, "You'll have to excuse the mess. My mother is staying with me for a little while. She and her boyfriend had an argument and she asked if she could stay with me until they sorted things out," Charleston shared.

"It's okay. I don't mind a little mess," I smiled sincerely.

Charleston seemed simultaneously nervous and excited. After pushing open the door, he stepped aside for me to enter the house. I stepped into the living area. It was nicely furnished: an off-white, overstuffed sofa and loveseat were placed against adjacent walls of one another; beautiful, large glassed coffee and end tables were positioned in front of and on the sides of the sofa; light-colored beige carpet covered the floors. I was impressed with his taste in furniture; albeit surprised. I would have expected him to have chosen furniture that was more contemporary.

Charleston escorted me up the stairs.

"I have three bedrooms up here and this is the loft," he pointed in the direction of a large open space filled with a television and large sofa. "This was my niece's room when she lived with me, and this was my sister's room when she stayed here," Charleston stated as he took me into the rooms.

Both rooms looked as though they were awaiting the return of their occupants; they appeared occupied. Clothing was indiscriminately thrown about the rooms; the beds were unmade.

"I'm going to get rid of this furniture and replace it with new furniture throughout the house." Charleston said as we moved from the bedrooms to the loft. "Over here is the master bedroom. I gave it to my mother while she's here, since she is the queen of my life. It also has a master bath," he added.

Charleston swung open the door of the master bedroom. Purple, floral-printed sheers hung loosely from an ornate curtain rod. A queen-sized bed was positioned on one wall and a large dresser and armoire on the others. Beautiful women's clothing lay scattered throughout the room: on the floor, on the dresser, and a large pile was pushed to one side of the bed.

"Come on! Come look!" Charleston urged enthusiastically.

I did not want to fully enter the bedroom. I felt like I was intruding on his mother's personal space.

"Come on! The bathroom has a separate shower and bath."

Charleston pointed out excitedly.

The strong scent of perfume permeated the air. Make-up stains covered the counters of the sink.

"Come on! Let me show you to my room. I'm sleeping downstairs in the guest room until Hattie leaves." Charleston said, affectionately referring to his mother.

We walked back down the stairs and into his room. An enticingly comfortable-looking, full-sized bed and a 32" television and stand occupied most of the space in the quaint room. Charleston's vast amount of clothes poured out of the small closet in the room. Across from his bedroom, on the opposite side of the hall, was another closet filled with his clothes. He was truly a fashionista.

I felt uncomfortable bringing my luggage into his room. My suitcase was so large that it looked like I was moving into his home permanently. However, I had nowhere else to place it, so I set the large luggage on the floor at the end of the bed where I hoped it would look as inconspicuous as possible.

After I showered, I peeled back the comforter and lay on the fluffy bed, until, within minutes, I was sound asleep.

~~~

I believed that I loved her at first sight. She was beautiful: rich, dark, ebony-colored skin, well-styled hair, impeccably dressed, southern, and, like Mother, she was from Alabama. In many ways, she reminded me of both of my grandmothers: funny, classy, gracious, and down-to-earth. She loved to talk, and I loved to listen to her. She shared the details of her life with me as though we had known each other all of our lives, which I assumed was her way with nearly everyone whom she met. She had a way of making one feel at home in her presence.

"So, now Christapha," she said in her southern dialect. "Now, what brings you this way?" She asked inquisitively.

Charleston chimed in before I could speak, "Mom, I told you that he was having trouble at school! You know how those White folks are."

"Chile, you ain't got to tell me! Them damn peckerwoods I work with somethin' else! But I don't take no mess from them! No, not Hattie Shears!" She smiled beautifully, exposing a gap between her two front teeth.

"Mom, tell him about the time when you let that supervisor of yours have it!!!" Charleston laughed heartily as Ms. Hattie began to tell one of her many stories. I sat on the sofa in pure delight and amazement with everything that she had been through and the beautiful woman that she had maintained, despite the horrific experiences of her life.

~~~

It happened, again. After just four weeks of living in Tracy, Charleston and I had decided to enter into a romantic relationship. Our choice seemed logical: we meshed well together. Our every waking moment was spent in one another's company, as I was unemployed and Charleston had taken a leave of absence from his job as a flight attendant, due to his father's passing the previous year.

Without the confines of work schedules, Charleston and I took leisurely drives to the Bay Area visiting his friends in Oakland and exploring San Francisco. We trekked across the Golden Gate Bridge, where the cool breeze soothingly caressed our skin and invigorated my soul. During our courtship, I had also discovered a hidden treasure of his: Charleston had a remarkable singing voice. I knew of no male singer that could compare to his vocal range and presentation of a song. His voice was the perfect blend of beauty, style, and soul. His vocal ability and delivery of a song reminded me of the great gospel singer Yolanda Adams.

Charleston appeared to be just what I needed to put my doomed relationship with Mally entirely behind me, as he was the complete antithesis of Mally in age, maturity, and experiences. Charleston was also modest to the extent of being somewhat prudish, which I needed in a partner in order for me to wholly heal.

Prior to the consummation of our relationship, for months, Charleston would sleep fully-clothed in his nightclothes in my bed with me. With the exception of times when he caressed my back to help me to sleep, he did not touch me in an inappropriate manner. I could tell that he loved and desired me sexually, yet he remained chaste. I, in turn, appreciated his modesty.

In juxtaposition to Mally, Charleston was a priest. And, while I would not have referred to Mally as a whore, I would have said that he did not place a high premium on sexual relations. Mally thought little to nothing about kissing, masturbating, or participating in fellatio with someone whom he barely knew. Charleston valued the sanctity of love and of love-making.

In addition to Charleston's virtuosity, he was a good guy. He was caring and compassionate, and he always went above and beyond himself to please me. Yet, despite my love of Charleston, I was not yet in-love with him. I needed more time to heal from the disappointment and hurt of my failed relationship with Mally—however, before any such healing could occur, my relationship with Charleston had begun to experience woes.

~~~

Although Charleston and I had dated for six months prior to entering our relationship, I had not invested any time in getting to know him in his environment. In the comfort of my home in Davis, away from all who knew him, Charleston could be who he wanted to be; he could embellish stories without me being wise to his falsehoods. Though, in his environment, truths became known.

"Hi, Chris!" Michelle, Charleston's oldest sister, greeted.

Charleston was the youngest child of three children; his sister, Trina, was the middle child.

"Hey, Michelle!" I smiled warmly. I was fond of Michelle. In some ways, she reminded me of Mymomme. She was strong, quick-tempered, and quick to fight. For me, her temperament was indicative of having been emotionally wounded. Her tough act was an attempt of hers to camouflage the hurt she had suffered. At her core, however, she was tender and incredibly compassionate.

"How you doing?" She asked, sweetly.

"I'm good. I was just cleaning the loft," I replied.

"Aww, you are going to be all day!" Michelle said to me, and then turning to her husband, "John remember when Mom first got this house…"

The seemingly benign words slid from her tongue effortlessly.

Later that evening when Charleston had returned home from choir rehearsal, I questioned him.

"Charleston, Michelle and John came over earlier. They referred to your house as being Ms. Hattie's," I said, calmly.

His face hardened. "They have always said that. This is my house. My name is on the deed!" Charleston declared irritatingly.

I did not believe him; too many things did not make sense to me. I recalled my impression of the living room furniture when I first entered the house. The style of the furniture was something that a middle-aged woman would choose, not a young man. I also remembered Charleston's words when he showed me the master suite: 'I gave it to my mother while she's here, since she is the queen of my life…'

It was not Charleston's extension to 'give' his mother the master bedroom that had seemed odd to me; it was the appearance and the condition of the room that was unsettling. Feminine curtains draped the window, the counter in the bathroom was heavily stained with make-up, and the room was in complete disarray. Most visitors would not have regarded their benefactor's home so carelessly.

As much as I would have liked for the falsehoods to have ended with the ownership of the home, the more time that I spent with Charleston's family and friends, the more I became aware of his dishonesties.

"Meko, remember the time you put on my dress and shoes?!" Marcie laughed, referencing Charleston by his middle name.

My spine stiffened. Charleston looked at me through the corner of his eye. He laughed lightly.

Marcie continued, "Remember how you were walking in my heels?!" She laughed heartily. "You walked better in my damn shoes than I did!" Marcie laughed so fully that she was unaware of the look of agony on Charleston's face.

Months ago, when I lived in my apartment in Davis, I had asked Charleston if he had ever worn women's clothing. In his usual haughty manner, he responded that he had not. My question was innocent. I held no judgment of a guy wearing women's clothing. One of my best friends was transgendered.

It seemed common to me for most males to try on women's apparel at some point in their lives. As children, my cousins and I had playfully donned my mother's wigs. As I grew older, I witnessed a number of men dressed as women on Halloween, most of whom, if not all, I assumed were heterosexuals. Wearing women clothing was simply not a big issue for me; however, being untruthful was unacceptable, no matter how miniscule the falsity.

As time progressed, I soon learned of a number of other lies that Charleston had told me; one of which threatened to collapse our relationship.

"Hey, Meko!" A tall, dark-skinned guy beamed. His eyes brightened at the sight of Charleston.

"How are you?" Charleston responded crisply to the guy. I knew the tone of Charleston's voice all too well. Yet, I said nothing. Charleston and I continued to walk along the semi-busy street of Oakland as if he had not seen the guy. "That was James. I knew him from church," Charleston offered.

"Oh, okay." I responded indifferently. Although I noticed the exchange between the guy and Charleston, I thought nothing of it until we were in Charleston's car on the way to his home and I was able to better process what I saw.

Charleston's demeanor and response to the guy was different than the way that he usually greeted people. Charleston was very amicable. He loved to be around people, laughing and joking with them. While I had seen him speak rudely to people before, he rarely did so with someone whom was obviously very fond of him. The guy apparently knew Charleston well, for he referred to him by his middle name; a name reserved only for Charleston's family members and close friends. Yet, Charleston responded to the guy as though he was a business acquaintance with whom he had bad dealings.

"Who did you say the guy was that we passed in the Square?" I asked.

"Uhh, James…" He replied nervously.

"Why were you upset with him?" I asked.

"Huh?" He feigned naiveté.

"You heard me."

"That was Anthony," he confessed.

"Anthony? The guy that you were in a relationship with?"

"Yes."

"Well, why did you say his name was James?"

"His middle name is James."

"Nigga, don't play those damn games with me! Yo' ass was trying to throw me off by calling him James! You've never referred to him by his middle name in the past! I'm getting tired of yo' got damn lies and half, mutha-fuckin' truths!" I exploded. My anger was not in Charleston speaking to Anthony. I would have expected him to speak to someone he once loved. My anger was rooted in his being deceitful about who Anthony was.

"I didn't lie." Charleston replied defensively.

"Nigga, you did lie! You gone tell me his name is some damn James, knowing damn well I knew of him by his first damn name! I'm getting' sick of yo' damn shit! Yo silly ass lie about every got damn thing! You lie about a damn house that ain't yours; you lie about muthafuckin' cars that you don't own; you lie about women's clothes and mutha fuckas that you used to like! I don't know what to believe out yo' got damn mouth! I'm getting' out of this bullshit of a relationship!" I raged.

I cursed, hollered, and yelled until we reached his home in Tracy an hour and a half from where we had just come. I walked directly into his room and began packing my clothes. I could not be with someone who lied. It was too much work. I did not know what I could believe and what I could not. My mind operated on high speed as was, I did not need anything extra to send it into over-drive.

"Please don't leave me, Chris!" Charleston beseeched, as he grabbed and pulled on my arm like a damsel in distress.

"Git yo' damn hands off me!" I yelled, nearly sounding like Shug Avery in *The Color Purple*.

I had never experienced anything so bizarre. I did not know if he was serious or not, but yanking and pulling on me was not the solution. He behaved like a crazed person on *The Jerry Springer Show*.

"Don't leave me! You are the best thing that happened to me!" He sobbed.

I also had never seen a grown man cry in such a manner. He looked like a child whom had his bicycle stolen from him. I was livid with him for having consistently lied to me, but I was not a cruel person. I broke.

"Listen, I don't like people lying to me," I said as gently as I could, considering, on a scale from one to ten, I was just at a ten. "I don't care about none of the crap you lied about! You lying about houses and shit! I rented a damn apartment. What in the hell do I care about whether you own your own house or if someone else owns it?! Cars and shit! I ain't even got a damn car, and you lying about whether you own or lease one! That's some silly shit! Somebody else may care about that materialistic shit, but I don't," I said emphatically.

Charleston continued to cry. I had absolutely never seen anything like what I was experiencing. And, he had the audacity to cry big, crocodile tears! If Charleston was faking his grief, he truly deserved an Academy Award for best performance ever in any category!

I walked from the bedroom and into the family room and sat down on the sofa. As Charleston continued to offer his heartfelt apologies, an image flashed before my eyes. *We were in the kitchen of my apartment in Davis. I stood at the entryway of the kitchen. Charleston stood near the stove ranting and raving arrogantly about nothing when I heard a small Voice say, "Don't get in a relationship."*

I laughed aloud at the admonishment of the Voice. I had absolutely no intention of being in a relationship with Charleston. At that time, I did not know Charleston well enough to enter a relationship with him. While he seemed like a cool-enough-guy in some ways; in other ways, he was incredibly arrogant. I despised arrogance and conceit. Entering a relationship with him seemed to be the unlikeliest of occurrences in my life; yet, several months later, there I was—not only was I in a relationship with Charleston, but I was also a fraction of a second from being in-love with him.

If I had known what was good for me, I would have risen from the sofa, finished packing my things, offered my condolences, and left Charleston's house…Ms. Hattie's house…or whoever's house—never to return! But I did not know what was good for me. I was a fool for love. I had not yet gained the wisdom to know when to leave a relationship.

I would soon learn that, just as it took far more than flour to bake a cake, it would take more than simply love to sustain our relationship.

Charleston had returned to back to work after his leave of absence had expired. He had not exited the front door of the house for more than five minutes when Ms. Hattie asked me to come upstairs to talk with her in the loft.

"I know what's going on? You got to get up pretty early to put one over on this old lady!" Ms. Hattie sneered in a Haitian accent immediately after I took a place on the sofa.

I knew what she was talking about as soon as she spoke the words.

"Ms. Hattie, I'm not trying to put anything pass you," I said wearily. I did not want to be involved in any mess that was not my own.

"I see everything. I just don't talk about everything I see!" She replied in a malicious near-whisper.

I knew the day was coming. I had conversation after conversation with Charleston, but to no avail. He consistently avoided talking to her.

"Ever since you came here, Meko been actin' different! He exercising, eating different, losing weight. I see how y'all look at each other; what y'all do for each other. Don't no friends just do that kinda stuff for each other! Y'all sleepin' in the same room with the door closed! I told Meko his ass better come from outta that room and sleep in one of them rooms upstairs!" Ms. Hattie fumed.

Another one of Charleston's lies. I had asked him why he had stopped sleeping in the room with me. He said that he did not want to wake me when he awakened to talk to Ms. Hattie before she left for work each morning.

"Ms. Hattie," I said calmly. "I wasn't trying to deceive you. I told Charleston he needed to talk to you."

"He ain't got no right bringing no mess like this up in my house!" She nearly shouted.

"I'm sorry, Ms. Hattie," I said soothingly.

I felt sympathy for her. Although I did not share most heterosexuals' negative view of homosexuality, I did understand how traumatizing the truth of a person's sexuality could be, especially for a parent. At birth, parents sometimes unintentionally poured into their children expectations of what they hoped them to be. Few, if any parents, envisioned their child being gay. Such knowledge would shatter not only their societal and/or religious beliefs of what is right and wrong, but also their own hopes for their children.

"What about them other ones? They tried to trick me, too?" She asked wonderingly, in reference to Charleston's friends.

"I don't want to say, Ms. Hattie. You have to talk to Charleston," I replied respectfully.

I could not disclose to Ms. Hattie the sexual orientations of Charleston's friends; though, in truth, I was baffled that she was not aware of Charleston or his friends' sexuality. It was not as though they were the epitome of masculinity and femininity. Charleston said "girl and chile" more than the average woman. His best friend wore eye liner faithfully and carried a "male" purse; and, some of his female friends were tougher than most guys in the roughest slums of any of America's housing projects.

"I can't believe them! Not a one of y'all said nothin'!" She said angrily and hurtfully at the same time.

"I'm sorry. I didn't mean to deceive you," I apologized, again.

I wanted to be left out of the deceit that Charleston had perpetuated. I was open about every facet of my life. I had no need, nor the desire to deceive anyone.

She raised her head and looked at me through grief-stricken eyes, "I know you didn't, Christapha."

~~~

In the following days, weeks, and months, Ms. Hattie alternated between being kind and mean toward me. At times, I was her best friend; and, at other times, she deplored my existence. Although

Charleston had been practicing homosexuality for many years before he knew me, Ms. Hattie believed that I was the reason that he was gay. She also felt that the truth of Charleston's sexual orientation and my relationship with him had been thrust upon her without any preparation. As she expressed to me, one minute she was being introduced to his "friend"; the next minute, she learned that he was gay. I wanted to tell her that I was not the cause of Charleston's sexuality, but my loyalty to Charleston prevented me from sharing any of the details of his sexuality with her.

I wholly understood Ms. Hattie's feelings. I was all too familiar with the sting of deceit. Had Charleston been forthright with me and told me that he shared a home with his mother, I would have never asked to stay with him, especially if I had known that she was unaware of his sexuality. I felt that Charleston should have said something to Ms. Hattie long before she had even the notion to approach me about his sexuality; yet, despite my many urgent pleas to him that he talk to her about his orientation and our relationship, he let things escalate until she felt betrayed, deceived, and resentful of our relationship and, ultimately, me.

Each subsequent event thereafter contributed to the downward spiral of my relationship with Charleston; though, rather than to terminate our relationship, I continued to move through it, dysfunctionally.

~~~

I enrolled in school at California State University, Hayward. I surmised, if UC Davis' graduate program did not give me the fundamental education in theater that I sought, I would acquire the knowledge at the baccalaureate level.

Midway through my first week as a student at CSU, I auditioned for a role in the play "Angels in America." The play dealt with the HIV/AIDS epidemic of the 1980s. It was an endearing and wonderfully written piece that not only examined the lives that were affected by the epidemic, but it also addressed homosexuality and the impact religion and/or ethnicity has on an individual's sexuality.

A day after auditioning for a role in the play, my name was posted outside of the theater amongst a list of cast members. I had gotten a role—or two! My characters were an imaginary travel agent and a former drag queen. The roles were minor, but I saw them as opportunities for me to exercise my skills and to gain recognition as an actor in the Bay Area's bustling theater community.

Chapter Seventeen

I received the call on a beautiful afternoon in October. Charleston and I had just moved into our apartment. We were snuggled warmly on the sofa in the den watching television.

"Luda, mama has just been transferred to hospice," Brandy said calmly on the other end of the phone.

"Huh?!" I asked worriedly.

"Yeah, they just took her a few minutes ago."

"Oh, no! Should I come home?" I asked in concern.

I really had no idea what hospice was. I understood that Aunt Carol's condition had worsened, but I lacked a full understanding of what her transfer to hospice entailed. In my limited knowledge of such events, I thought of hospice as a nursing home.

"No, she's fine. There's really not much you can do here," Brandy responded in her usual placid tone.

"Okay. I'll come home in a few weeks after this play ends. I love you."

"Mhm, love you, too."

The initial call came as a surprise; the second call, two days later, changed my world forever.

"Luda, Mama passed," Brandy sobbed softly into the phone.

My throat constricted involuntarily. The cell phone threatened to fall from my weakened hand. My heart pumped erratically beneath my shirt. I lifted my head as my eyes searched within the deepest blue of the sky for my aunt. Slow-moving tears flowed effortlessly from my eyes.

"Okay. Thank you for calling me. I love you," I said as I ended the call.

I stood perfectly still on the campus of CSU, Hayward as my mind and the world around me whirled. I felt a numbing coldness beneath my skin. Charleston stood at my side.

"Are you okay?" He asked, gently resting his hand on my shoulder.

I turned to look into his worried face. "Aunt Carol passed away."

I cried uncontrollably. Speaking the words made her death more real. He grabbed me close to him, hugging me soothingly.

"I'm okay," I muttered after a couple of minutes, though, in truth, I was not.

Nothing in life had prepared me for the finality of death. No one with whom I had shared an intimate relationship had died. I wobbled to Charleston's car on distrustful legs. I collapsed once inside the car as I tried to put together the pieces of my aunt's demise.

~~~

Life goes on after the death of a loved one, yet it does so painfully and slowly. Charleston and I flew to Toledo for my Aunt Carol's funeral services. We arrived the day of the wake. After quickly showering and dressing, Allen drove us to the funeral home to view Aunt Carol's body.

"You gone be all right, Kiss?" Allen asked in his familiar Jamaican accent.

The tone of his deep voice was laced with love and concern. I had never known him to sound so tender. He had always been the strong, domineering patriarch of my maternal family. Rarely, if ever, had he exhibited such sensitivity.

I turned to Allen before I exited Mama's minivan, we locked eyes. I looked pass the tint of his eyeglasses, beyond the blue-grayness of his cataracts through his spirit and into his soul. It was beautiful. All of the lessons of his incessant talks with me as a child culminated to that point. He had done well by me as a grandfather; he had fulfilled his divine purpose on earth with me. At that moment, if at no other time, I saw him for the gem that he was.

"Yes, I'll be all right," I smiled back as I stepped down from the minivan. "I love you."

The following day, Charleston, Mama, Mymomme, Geneva, Miah-Miah, and I crammed into Mama's minivan to attend the home-going service for my Aunt Carol. I did not want to be there, yet I sat on the hard wooden pew of the church, half-listening to the eulogy and the well-wishes of family-friends who were in attendance.

After Aunt Carol's casket had been closed, everyone in the church stood to view the casket as it was being carried to the hearse. The gravity of the moment descended upon me, again. My mind would not allow me to believe that, within the casket, lay my aunt. It was unfathomable. I could not believe that I would not see her standing in the kitchen with a cup of coffee resting on a nearby counter as circles of smoke filled the kitchen from her slow-burning cigarette. I would never see the easy glide of her short, bowed legs?! I would never ever see the soft brown of her eyes?!!!

The realization was too much for me. My knees buckled, my clinched throat relaxed enough to release my spirit's groan as tears flung from my eyes and down my face. Miah rushed to my side just as I lost my footing. It was all too unreal for me. I sobbed without restraint outside of the church as my younger brother supported my grief-stricken body, while the pallbearers carried Aunt Carol's casket from the old church and into the waiting black hearse.

Chapter Eighteen

The year had ended somberly. As hard as I tried, I just could not get pass Aunt Carol's death. The only joy I received came in a visit from Mymomme and my niece and nephew during the Christmas holiday. Charleston and I festively decorated our apartment in anticipation of their arrival. Ms. Hattie and Charleston's sisters went out of their way to make my family feel welcome by giving them presents for Christmas. Charleston's family's show of kindness toward my loved ones was what I needed to experience to get through the year and to move optimistically forward into the next one.

At the start of the year, I auditioned for a role in another play. The play, *Joe Turner's Come and Gone*, was written by August Wilson, a prolific African American playwright. Mr. Wilson had written ten plays that examined the lives of African Americans during each decade of the twentieth century.

I was assigned the role of a young, country boy named Jeremy. The cast and I rehearsed six days a week for four weeks. I anxiously delved into my work in an effort to help to ease the grief that I felt over the loss of my aunt.

We opened the play during the first week of February in San Francisco at the Lorraine Hansberry Theater to sold-out crowds. Just as I had thought, performing was just what I needed to help me to deal with Aunt Carol's death. Performing aided me in connecting with the Creator through my artistic work.

Two weeks into the production, however, I received grave news. Allen had suffered a heart attack. I frantically made arrangements to fly back to Toledo to be with my family, though, before I could finalize the arrangements, Allen called me on the phone from the hospital just as I was about to go onto the stage.

"Kiss?" Allen said into the receiver.

"Hey, granddaddy. How are you feeling?" I asked concerned.

"Ahh, you know me, Kiss! I'm gone be all right!" He said optimistically.

"Yeah?" I asked disbelievingly. "I'm coming home in a couple of days to check on you. I'm in a play and I don't have a replacement, so I can't leave today or tomorrow."

"Naw, Kiss, you stay there and do what you gotta do, bruh. I'ma be all right!" Allen assured me.

"You sure? I don't want to lose you, granddaddy," I said forlornly.

Seldom did I refer to Allen by anything other than his first name. My cousins and I had been raised to call him by his first name just as our mothers had called him. My love of him had become so great that merely calling him by his birth name did not always seem appropriate; as though his simple name did not communicate the depth of my love for him.

"Aww, man, you know me! I'm a Mandingo Warrior!" He joked.

Since surviving the atrocities of prison, I had jokingly come to refer to myself as a Mandingo Warrior. Allen, identifying with the greatness within himself, began to call himself a warrior of the African tribe as well. It had become a long-standing point of humor between us.

I laughed aloud. "Okay, granddaddy. Then, I'll see you in a couple weeks when the play ends."

"You got it, grandson! Hey, Kiss, bring yo' clippers wit you to cut my hair when you here!" He said before disconnecting the call.

I smiled from ear to ear as I went back into the dressing room to finish preparing for the show. I marveled at being able to receive Allen's call. Generally, I did get cell phone reception in the dressing room. I innately shrugged my shoulders, thinking that God had given me the blessing that I needed to get through my performance.

~~~

Charleston and I awakened rather late on a Wednesday morning. The voice message came in around seven a.m. EST. I grabbed the phone from the nightstand and began listening to the recording.

"Christafa, baby, this yo' granny. Yo' granddaddy done passed on, baby. Call me, baby, when you can, baby."

The phone fell from my hand. I jumped up from the bed, startling Charleston awake. I hurriedly exited the room, pacing around the living room. Charleston quickly came into the room.

"What's wrong?" He asked frantically.

"Allen's dead."

"Oh, no, I'm sorry," he said, stretching forth his arms, holding me in a tender embrace.

I wept like an infant child. I did not know what to do. I was nowhere near having dealt with Aunt Carol's passing and now my grandfather had passed away as well. I felt like my world was closing in on me.

~~~

Death was tragic to me. I had no understanding of its purpose. It was torture. I did not understand how God could allow us to love our loved ones only to have us separated from them until we ourselves died. It seemed cruel.

I replayed in my mind my last conversations with Allen…the last time I saw him. As with Aunt Carol, I could not imagine that I would never see him on earth, again.

I thought of the many times when I would fall asleep on the sofa in the living room and he would come home during the wee hours of the morning and fall asleep beside me in the reclining chair. I would awaken to the sound of his labored breathing; my own breathing matching his. I felt connected with him, as though we were one: grandfather and grandson.

I remembered when my cousin, De-De, and I accompanied him to his hometown in Arkansas. The light of pride shone brightly in his eyes as he showed his grandsons the land on which he had been raised.

Memories. The mind that had served me well in school, agonized me in the wake of Allen's death. I could not forget the memories that we had forged.

~~~

Charleston and I had more than our share of heartaches, yet he never failed me during the deaths of my loved ones. He was always there to offer me support: firm, reassuring hugs; gentle touches of solace; consoling glances from across the room. He had become an unwavering presence of comfort.

The airline with whom Charleston worked allowed us to fly first-class to attend Allen's funeral service. As with Aunt Carol's services, Charleston and I arrived the day of the wake and one day before the funeral.

Soon after arriving to the Toledo, Charleston and I made our way to the funeral home. I had unfinished business with my granddaddy.

I drove Mama's Minivan to the funeral home. Sadly and ironically, the last time that I was at the funeral home, Allen had taken me to view Aunt Carol's body. Just four months later, I was there to see him for the last time.

As if guided by Allen's spirit, I walked to where his body laid. I looked down at him. He looked good in his dark, blue suit. The funeral home had done a wonderful job. He looked like his former self before arthritis had weakened his limbs and cardio vascular disease had robbed him of his thick, muscular build.

"Hey, granddaddy. I didn't forget you." I said as I gently touched his hand.

I set the black bag on a nearby chair and looked for an electrical outlet. I plugged the clippers into the electrical socket.

"Not too much off the top, Kiss. It's gettin' low up there." Allen whispered in my ear before I cut the crown of his hair, as he had said many times before in the past.

A cool breeze flowed through the room. Goosebumps rose on my arms. The air carried the scent of Old Spice. I felt a slight pressure against my arm. I smiled as a single tear cascaded from my eye.

"I love you," I whispered to him.

~~~

"Each of us has a purpose to fulfill while we are here on earth," I said from the podium. "Whatever we are most remembered for is the thing that we most represented while we are here on earth. Some of us are comical and so it is our humor for which we are known; others of us kind-hearted and so it is our kindness for which we are most remembered. Allen was strong. It was his strength for which he is most remembered. He was not only strong physically but he was strong mentally, emotionally, and spiritually. He passed those strengths on to us; his family." I stopped abruptly to compose myself, as my throat constricted and tears filled my eyes.

"Allen would ask us not to cry, not to mourn his passing, but I am. I love him and I miss him. Crying is not an indication of weakness to me; it is an indication that he was loved, that his life meant something. I wrote a poem which I published in a book that I wrote. The poem is entitled 'Today'. I believe it captures the essence of who Allen was. Allen lived everyday as though it was his last. 'Today' encourages us to make the most of each day that we are given."

The attendees clapped their hands wildly after I read the poem. I took a seat next to my family. I was satisfied. I had expressed the love of my heart and the gratitude that I felt to a man who had served me well as a grandfather.

~~~~

Charleston and I rushed from the cemetery to the airport to fly back to California. As with before, I had no replacement to cover my absence in the play. We arrived back in California the day before my performance. I was a bit uncertain as to how I would perform; if I could handle the stressfulness of performing in light of my circumstances.

As always, I said a prayer before stepping onto the stage. I delivered all of my lines well until I arrived at the end of a scene. In the play, my character had experienced the death of a loved one. As I began to deliver my lines, I thought of Allen. I saw his face before my eyes; the sun of his smile, I stumbled, unsure of what to say. I looked into the eyes of my cohort as she stood before me, waiting for me to deliver the next line of the play. As I looked in her eyes, I felt the spirit of my granddaddy.

"I'm gone be all right, Kiss," Allen whispered. I smiled sweetly, content. I continued where I left off from the script.

If the audience was aware of my mishap, it was not mentioned. They applauded loudly as my name was said at the end of the play; giving me an added sense of peace and pride for my performance, despite the loss of my beloved granddaddy.

Each of the remaining six performances went smoothly. My performance during the play was so well received that I was asked to be in another play which began the following week. I happily accepted the offer; however, the few short days between the plays did not work in my favor. The down time gave my mind an opportunity to fully absorb my loss. I sank into a deep depression from which I thought I would never recover.

~~~

Grief consumed me. My mind melded Aunt Carol and Allen's deaths together. I was overwhelmed. I had lost all will to live. And, then, they came to me.

I lay in my bed crying when Aunt Carol appeared to me. She wore a white, loose-fitting gown. Her hair was cut short; soft, black curls framed her face perfectly. Her naturally flawless, honey brown skin was even more radiant. Her still petite frame was fuller, healthier in death.

"What's wrong, Chris?" She asked compassionately.

I looked at her through tear-filled eyes. "I didn't get a chance to see you before you left, and I never paid you the twenty dollars you let me borrow when I was sixteen."

I began to sob, again. "Boy, that's all!" She chided with her hand on her hip.

"Yea...I miss you. I didn't know that you would leave." My voice shook violent with each word that I spoke.

"Awww, Chris, it's okay. I'm here now." She said soothingly.

She walked closer to me. My chest began to heave up and down in an effort to breathe through my sobs. Aunt Carol bent down to hug me. I looked into her face, smiling. Just as her spirit transfused into my own, I awakened with a start, bathed in sweat and tears.

Days later, Allen appeared.

He was in a seated position in thin air. Pitch blackness surrounded him on every side. He appeared to be in a tunnel. The only visible light radiated from him.

"Allen, what's it like there?" I asked.

His death had challenged my understanding of life and death. I had been raised as a Christian, yet the various stories of life after death conflicted with one another. I did not know whether they were in Heaven or if they were in a holding cell of sorts awaiting the return of Christ. I just did not know.

"It's quiet; real quiet." His voice reverberated, as though he was in a cave or underwater.

I tried to adjust my eyes so that I could see him more clearly. He was so far away from me.

"I don't like this; I don't know if I can go on..." I said in dismay.

He face suddenly appeared closer to me. He, like Aunt Carol, looked great. His charcoal-black skin glistened. The light beneath his skin or within him shined through brilliantly, giving him a translucent appearance.

"You gone be all right." His voice echoed around me.

Chapter Nineteen

After the spiritual-dreams with Aunt Carol and Allen, I felt exhilarated, as if my deceased loved ones had given me what I needed to continue moving forward. I greeted each day with the same enthusiasm that I had before their passings, yet with a different understanding of life and our purposes on Earth. I was in awe of God and His magnificence. He had never failed me. During every struggle in my life, he had always sent me encouragement to aid me during my journey.

However, just as my life had begun to move in the right direction mentally and spiritually, my relationship with Charleston had reclaimed its downward spiral. We argued about everything. We tried our best to go twenty-fours without bickering; though, more often than not, we failed.

The truth of the matter was that Charleston and I were not truly friends. I fell in love with Charleston without knowing wholly who he was as a person. My initial feelings for him were rooted in the person that he showed me in Davis. After I looked pass his arrogance, I was able to see that he was incredibly funny, kind, and very attentive to my needs and wants; however, another part of Charleston's personality was markedly different than the man I had chosen to love.

I admitted to myself that a huge part of my choice to enter into a relationship with Charleston was based, not only on his show of love toward me, but also on the fact that Charleston was everything that Mally was not. I had not healed enough from my relationship with Mally to be able to make a healthy decision of whether to enter into a romantic relationship with someone else. As such, my relationship with Charleston was based on the failure of my relationship with Mally, which created a faulty foundation, to express the least. The truthfulness of my assertion, coupled with Charleston's dishonesty, was disastrous for the relationship. We needed honesty, effective communication, and a true understanding of one another in order for our relationship to have endured the trials of romanticism.

~~~

Despite my understanding of the issues in our relationship, I made an attempt to make amends with Charleston and to reconcile our relationship. Perhaps, I should have gone about it in a different manner. Maybe I could have saved the extra words for a soliloquy and only shared my thoughts that were necessary for him to hear. I did not, however. Instead, I began the conversation talking about the many things that Ms. Hattie had done to sabotage our relationship. He, in return, had become incensed.

"I'm tired of hearing what my mother has done!" Charleston said in a tone of annoyance.

I had always heard it said that hindsight is 20/20. After reviewing the situation, I could see how I should have remained calm. After all, I was speaking to him about his mother's misbehavior. It was true. Ms. Hattie was always doing or saying something crazy toward us. And, I, in turn, berated him about how he allowed her to mistreat us. Any person who loves his mother would have gotten tired of hearing someone talk about all the negative things that his mother has done toward him and his partner, but my anger did not allow me to think objectively. Instead, I behaved senselessly.

"Nigga, I don't give a fuck what you tired of hearing! It ain't no damn way I'd let my mama or anybody else for that matter come against my damn relationship! You a weak, spineless ass nigga! Now, if she left her damn shoes in the living room, your goofy ass would be quick to chide, 'Mom! Why can't you keep up with your stuff...I'm getting' tired of picking up behind you!' In your arrogant ass, White lady tone, but let her ass say something to or about us and yo' ass act like a scared ass kindergartner!"

"I'm not listening to this one minute longer!" He seethed, throwing the comforter back and jumping up from the bed.

"I bet yo' ass gone listen to it as long as you in my muthafuckin' face!" I yelled.

Charleston rushed to the closet to get dressed. However, before doing so, he flicked on the lamp that sat on the nightstand. The bright light blinded me. I quickly reached for the lamp to turn off the light, but he snatched the lamp from the nightstand before I could get to it. Lividly, I jumped to my feet and yanked the lamp from his hand. He pushed me.

Whatever semblance of sanity that I might have had was gone. It was as though all of the anger and disappointment that I had felt over the last year of our relationship had come to a head. I recalled all of the lies Charleston had told me. I remembered the days and nights that I had listened to his stories of abuse, and how I had tried to heal the wounds of his past with the love of my soul. I relived the assaults that Ms. Hattie had flung at me, at us; I re-experienced his best friend's attempts to insult me; and, the isolation that I suffered from his church family. I thought of how he lacked the courage to defend me or our union.

In two deft movements, I threw him from one area of the bedroom to the next area until we were in the master bathroom. I slung him around in the bathroom several times and then tossed him back into the bedroom where the altercation had begun. Still not satisfied, I grabbed his head, thrashing it violently into a wall.

I was outraged. I breathed in and out like an enraged bull ready to pounce on a matador. I grabbed the sides of his head once more, intent on making it meet the wall behind him again, yet, before I could do anymore harm to him, I suddenly stopped myself. I was spent. I had no more to give to the relationship: no more good; no more bad. All of the hurt that I had endured over the months of our relationship was gone. I quietly surrendered as I collapsed on the floor beside Charleston.

A few short minutes after the altercation, I rose from the floor and lay on the bed. Charleston lay beside me. He reached for me. He touched me seductively as he moved closer to me, attempting to kiss me. I gently pushed him away from me, mildly reproaching his attempt to make love.

Although, I was proud of myself for presumably taking a stance against the abuse I had suffered while I was in the relationship with Charleston, I was simultaneously ashamed of myself. Yes, I had finally rebuked the pain and mistreatment that I had endured; however, in doing so, I had inflicted bodily pain to my partner—the person whom I supposedly loved.

I did not believe in fighting in romantic relationships. To me, the act of fighting went against the very premise on which the relationship was established—love. I did not believe that true love could exist in violence. Not only was my behavior a contradiction to love I felt for Charleston, the volatility in which I behaved could have seriously injured or killed him, as any one of the blows to his head could have caused his brain to hemorrhage.

Fighting was not the solution to my unhappiness.

"Charleston, we can't do this…we can't make love after what just happened. Do you realize that I could have killed you? This is not the way that two people who are in love with one another act. We need to see a therapist," I suggested.

Charleston had been reared in an emotionally and physically abusive home. Subconsciously, it seemed to me that his understanding of romantic relationships that were unhealthy was to continue in them, despite the volatile nature of the relationship. While I, too, had been raised in a dysfunctional, abusive family, I had the wherewithal to know that abuse in any relationship was not okay. Abuse was not something that one just swept under the rug, per se, as though it never occurred. The abusive act had to be examined and some sort of resolution had to be met, even if that meant ending the relationship; yet, to behave as if the violation did not occur was dangerous.

Charleston did not respond to what I said. He simply listened. Then, in one quick movement, he moved to his side of the bed.

~~~

After the fight with Charleston, our relationship had gone on much as it had prior to the fight. We still constantly bickered with one another; we still disagreed on most things; we still argued incessantly. We copulated far less frequently and, during the times that we did, the glow of lovemaking was short-lived. Before long, we were back to our usual dysfunctional routine with one another.

I knew that it would be a matter of time before I would leave the relationship. The fight should have been the finale for me, though it was not. I had not lived in dysfunction with Charleston long enough to definitively end the relationship.

"Who is that texting you after midnight?" I asked suspiciously.

"Probably Willie." Charleston responded, referring to his best friend.

A Voice told me to check his phone. I did not believe in rummaging through anyone's phone for any reason, not even a dishonest partner, yet I felt drawn toward the phone. Under normal circumstances, I would have simply ignored the late-night text, but those were not normal times.

I walked into the bedroom from the bathroom and retrieved Charleston's phone from off of the nightstand.

"'Call me,'" the message stated. "Uh, this is not a message from Willie. This is an unfamiliar area code," I said to him.

He rushed into the bedroom to retrieve his phone. My suspicions were heightened. He tried to snatch his phone from my hand. I used one of my arms to keep him at bay and the other to manipulate the buttons of his phone. Using my thumb, I scrolled through the messages between Charleston and the unknown person.

"Who is this?! It's from a 206 area code?" I asked.

"It's my best friend," Charleston replied.

"What?! Do I look like a damn fool?! Willie's your best friend and this ain't his number!"

"It's from Carl. We've been best friends since I was a teenager. He's straight and married."

"Nigga, if he's your best friend, why haven't I ever heard of him or seen him in all the time that I've known you?! And, why isn't his number saved, if he's your 'best friend'?"

I read several of the messages.

"This don't sound like no messages from a best friend and definitely not a "straight" best friend! And, why would his married, straight ass text you at one o'clock in the damn morning?! Nigga, you lying again!" I laughed.

Strangely, for some reason, I was not upset. Perhaps, I saw Charleston's presumed act of infidelity as a way out of the relationship. Senselessly, I did not have the good sense to leave the relationship for all of the reasons that had occurred in the past. I needed something a little more substantial, as though lying and fighting were not enough.

"I'm not lying. He's my best friend!" Charleston whined.

He sounded like a spoiled child, which made the situation even more comical to me. I made a game of the farce by refusing to give his phone to him. He chased me all around the apartment, until I ran outside where he continued to give chase. I taunted and teased him merciless for twenty minutes or so.

I knew that I was behaving immaturely, but I did not care. I had grown weary of usually being the mature, rationally-minded person in the relationship.

Eventually, I gave him his phone, though not before I took the keys to one of his cars. We played another game of cat and mouse, until I had grown tired of that childish game, too. I placed his keys in the pocket of my robe and got into bed to go to sleep. Charleston angrily left our apartment.

A short time later, I heard a tap at the front door, followed by another tap on the bedroom door.

"Yeah," I shouted from the bed.

"Police, open the door, please." A male voice said authoritatively.

What? I know damn well he did not call the police! I grabbed my robed from the edge of the bed where I had tossed it. After putting on my robe, I opened the bedroom door.

"Sir, we received a phone call from this gentleman who stated that you have his car keys."

I looked at the officer matter-of-factly, "Yes?"

"Would you like to explain to me what's going on?"

I looked at the other officer and then to Charleston who stood next to him. *This is not the part of his plan that he had predicted.* Charleston shifted from one leg to the other. He was uncomfortable. He was not yet able to talk openly about his sexuality.

"Yeah," I said assuredly. *This is apparently what Charleston wanted, since it was his decision to call the police.* Instead of looking at the officer as I spoke, I looked directly into Charleston's eyes. "My partner and I," I said placing particular emphasis on the word 'partner'.

"…were in the bathroom preparing to retire for the evening when I heard his cell phone chime, an indication that he had received a message. Since it was already after midnight, I wondered who could be calling him at such an hour." I paused for a moment, though without breaking my focus on Charleston. "After checking his phone, I realized that the message was from an unsaved number. As a scrolled through the messages, I learned that my partner and the person whom had texted after midnight had been sending messages to one another over the past couple of weeks. Some of the messages simply stated, 'Call me!' while others contained sentiments such as, 'miss you…sorry, call back….need to talk to you'. The messages hardly seemed like messages from Charleston's best friend as he had claimed. Irritated with yet another one of his lies, I withheld his phone from him and, later, I took the keys to his car." I stated calmly as I broke eye contact with Charleston and looked at the officer.

If looks could kill, I would have been dead and in my grave. Charleston was seething as he stood to the right of the officer.

"Well, sir," the officer began uncomfortably as he cleared his throat. "Uh, well, I'm sorry you had to go through that, but you have to give Mr. Shears back his keys. It's his property, sir."

"Of course," I replied unfazed, as I reached in the pocket of my robe to get the keys.

"Thank you, sir." The officer said as I handed him the keys.

I nodded my head to the officer in acceptance of his politeness. I looked over to Charleston who simultaneously had a look of anger and defeat on his face. I did not know what he expected my response to be to the officers' presence. I had served seven and a half years in prison surrounded by seventy correctional officers who made it their business to make our existence as inmates a living hell. Surely, he could not have thought that merely the appearance of an officer or two would get me riled. It would take far more effort than that to ruffle my feathers.

Charleston did not return home for several days after our fiasco. During which time, I made arrangements to acquire a car of my own. His absence gave me the space to think more freely on the state of our relationship and my need to terminate it. Although I accepted full responsibility for my immature behavior leading to the police intervention, I also had the wherewithal to know that the mayhem would not have begun had Charleston not received a text message late in the evening from his supposed best friend.

Things were different between Charleston and I after he returned home; not so much on his end, though for me, each subsequent negative further strengthened my resolve to end the relationship. For the time being, the relationship continued as best it could under the weight of dysfunction.

Our apartment lease soon expired. We chose not to renew our lease. We were unable to afford our monthly expenses. The price of our rent had increased. Although Charleston was working regularly, his pay was not enough to support our monthly expenses, and I was unemployed. Despite having achieved both an Associates and Bachelor's degree, work was difficult to acquire as an ex-felon.

With nowhere to go, we placed my furniture in a storage facility and we moved back into Ms. Hattie's home with her. Ms Hattie was extremely elated to have Charleston back living in the house with her. She was in great spirits for all of a week and, unsurprisingly, her dormant behavior resumed to its previous state of craziness.

Just when I knew that I could take no more, I decided to move to leave. Determined to place the relationship behind me, I quickly packed my clothes early one December morning and loaded them into my car. After taking a short nap, I jumped into my car with Atlanta as my final destination.

Once in Atlanta, I began thinking about the course in which my life was to take. I was not yet ready to relinquish my pursuit of acting. Acting had become my passion. I needed to see what the end would be. I decided to stay in Atlanta with my daddy for a couple of months. During which time, I would acquire a job and save enough money so that I could return to California. However, as fate would have it, three weeks from my arrival to Georgia, I received an email for a job that I had applied to shortly before I left California.

I was offered a position as a residential manager at a homeless shelter for HIV+ residents. I graciously accepted the position from nearly 3000 miles away, ensuring the hiring manager that I would be ready to begin work on the third of January.

After three weeks of being in Atlanta, I was on the road to California, again. This time, however, I was armed with a plan.

I made the trek to California in two days. During my time in Georgia, Charleston and I had presumably made amends. However, just days after being in Tracy in his home with Ms. Hattie, I soon learned that nothing had changed between us. We simply were not meant to be together as lovers.

Ms. Hattie was incensed that I had returned. She had begun to get used to the ideal that I was gone from Charleston's life.

"You see, when I say I'm going to do something, I do it! I don't flip and flop once I make a decision. When I left Charleston (referring to Charleston Sr.), I didn't look back twice!" She declared emphatically, as a means of encouraging me to go back from whence I had come.

I smiled politely at her as she expressed her sentiments. She was correct. According to her own testimonies to me, once she had made the decision to leave Charleston Sr., for good, she stayed true to her resolve; however, it took thirty years for her to get to that point. She had failed at leaving an innumerable amount of times before she was finally able to firmly declare that enough was enough.

While Charleston and I were not technically in a relationship, we still loved one another. We tried to get along and to make our relationship work, but it was too late. Too much damage had been done.

I had grown stronger and wiser while in Georgia. I refused to go back to the unhealthy relationship that was ours. Realizing that things would remain the same until I made a significant change, I moved from their home and into my car.

My choice to be homeless was bold. I was 3000 miles from the family with whom I had been raised. I was in an unfamiliar state and town. However, I surmised that I needed to do what was best for me mentally, emotionally, and spiritually. I could not remain in a household where my partner's mother constantly attacked and blamed me for something that was not my doing; nor could I remain in a romantic relationship that was dysfunctional.

During the day, I slept in my car in the parking lot of CSU's campus; at night, I worked twelve hour shifts at the homeless shelter.

Every day after I left work, and sometimes three hours before my shift began in the evening, I worked-out at a local gym where I was a member. After I completed my exercise regimen, I showered and changed into clean clothing.

My supervisor, after learning that I was residing in my car, offered me one of the rooms at the homeless facility. I declined her offer, yet I accepted her extension to use the washer and dryer that was provided for the residents, so that I could wash my laundry. During the six weeks that I lived in my car, I survived on Subway's five-dollar foot-long sub-sandwiches, IHOP's pancake and omelet entrées, and I regularly purchased oranges, apples, and filtered water from the grocery store.

After being back in California for two months, I had saved enough money to make the move to Los Angeles. Even though my relationship with Charleston had altered drastically, I still loved him. I had not been blessed with the fortitude to simply walk away from a relationship. Perhaps, the unhealthy ways that Mama, Mymomme, and my aunts loved their men had seeped into my being and tainted my sound judgment. It seemed that I had rather live in the tattered house that our relationship had become, than to wholly accept that some things cannot be repaired.

Once again, I suggested to Charleston that we get counseling to mend our severely broken relationship. I even offered to commute from Los Angeles to Oakland on a regular basis to maintain some semblance of a relationship. I tried with every fiber of my being to make our relationship work when in my heart I knew that it was best to let it go. I had truly done all that I could; all that I knew to do to keep the relationship afloat. Until, finally, I resolved in my spirit that the time had come for me to make my transition to Los Angeles without Charleston and the unnecessary weight of our tumultuous relationship.

Chapter Twenty

The city of angels was different. It was not the same city that it was when I had arrived there nearly three years ago after graduating from B.G. It looked different. Its energy was different—or so it seemed.

As I pondered the assumed changes in the city, I realized that the city was not different. The change lay in me. I was a very different person than I was three years ago when I had first moved to California. I had overcome the deaths of two very special people to me. I had endured the ups and downs of a turbulent relationship. My personal and professional aspirations had been violently assaulted. Yet, there I stood in the city of dreams, strong and unwilling to accept defeat.

Within two weeks of arriving in Los Angeles, I had secured a talent agent. Two months later, I began working at the Los Angeles Gay and Lesbian Center as a health educator. The division under which I worked was named Positive Awareness. It was our division's responsibility to educate and counsel the Center's HIV-positive clientele on ways of living healthily, in spite of their statuses. As health educators, we encouraged our clients to live authentically, we instructed them of the dangers of engaging in unprotected sex as persons living with HIV, and we gave them the skills to accept and to cope with their conditions. We also offered one-on-one counseling sessions within the scope of our expertise, education, and training.

I still had no home of my own; however, my cousin, Diane, allowed me to live with her again until I was able to find a place of my own. Although, I slept on the floor of her living room, I was grateful to have somewhere to lay my head. As with before when Diane welcomed me into her house, I felt at home. She and I had a quiet understanding and love for one another. We did not spend a great deal of time together, yet the moments that we shared were special. I listened intently as she told me stories of her childhood in Missouri with her grandmother (my great-grandmother), her former marriage, and the joys and pains of being a mother and grandmother, virtually alone. I secretly added her to the list in my heart of people that I would remember when God blessed me financially. She deserved a break. Few people maintained the goodness of the Creator in spite of heartaches and disappointments, yet she had found the strength and courage to do so while raising four wonderful children and a host of grandchildren.

~~~

My days in Los Angeles were numbered. I had only been there for five short months when I received the call.

"Son, your grandmother isn't doing well. She has congested heart failure and she has cancer near her breast bone as well. You need to come home to see about her," my daddy expressed solemnly into the phone receiver.

What, not Mother, as well?! I could not believe that I was experiencing yet another loss. I did not know if I could bare the grief of death.

"Okay. I'll make arrangements with my job to leave in a couple of days."

After the phone call with my daddy, I walked up the stairs to the department to request a few days off from work. However, before I could open the door to my department, my cell phone rang, again. I quickly grabbed it from the holster on my hip. I looked down at the caller identification. The phone call was from my aunt, Geneva. I talked on the phone to Geneva or Brandy every morning while I drove to work. Since I had talked with Brandy on the drive to work that morning, I had failed to converse with Geneva.

"Hey, Chrissie Boo."

"Hey, Geneva! Give me one second, bae." I said hurriedly into the phone receiver. "I'm just about to walk into work. I'll call you right back after I get situated."

"Okay. Don't forget. It's important," she urged.

"Okay. I won't," I replied.

I sat my water bottle and client files down on my desk before I rushed back out of the office to return Geneva's call. She sounded particularly distressed.

I walked back down the stairs to an area where I could talk to her freely without being overheard.

"Geneva? Okay, I'm back," I said, after the call was connected.

"You talk to anybody, yet?" She said in a conspiratorial tone.

"Uhn uh, about what?" I asked wonderingly.

"Mama sick. The doctors say she got cancer, but don't say

nothing. Rachel and 'nem don't want nobody to know," Geneva confided in reference to her older sisters.

"Oh, my God!" Tears began to instantly well into my eyes, clouding my vision. "Where is the cancer?"

"They don't know. They think it's in her stomach."

"Oh, God! I can't believe this…" I held my free hand to my head, trying to absorb the enormity of what she had said. "Okay. I'm coming home."

"Chrissie Boo, you gone be okay?" Geneva asked in concern.

"Yeah, I'll be okay." I said in between sniffles. "I'll call you back."

"Okay. I love you."

"Mm hmm, I love you, too," I said before I disconnected the call.

I paced around the lobby of the building several times. My mind whirled. I was overwhelmed. I felt like a cruel, twisted trick was being played on me. I could not handle losing both of my grandmothers. I could not.

As I turned to walk up the stairs, the phone rang.

"Hey. You hear about Mama?" Mymomme said into the receiver.

"Yeah, Geneva just told me," I said, absentmindedly having forgotten that Geneva asked me not to let anyone know that she told me about Mama's condition.

"Hmpf," she scoffed. "I shoulda known."

I could not deal with Mymomme's jealousy that Geneva had shared the news with me before she had the opportunity to tell me. I had too many other things going on to try to placate her.

"Mymomme, I have to go to talk to my supervisor. I'll call you back."

"Mhmm, okay," she replied scornfully.

I walked upstairs to my department. I spoke with my supervisor to tell him of my circumstances and that I would be resigning from my position. He was dismayed and instructed me to share the news with our department manager. While speaking with the department manager, she encouraged me to finish the work-week. I really did not want to stay in California any longer than a minute. I wanted to get home to my grandmothers; to my family. I did not want to lose another person while in California.

Yet, I did as I was advised and completed my exit examination at work. On Friday, I left California for Atlanta where I met my daddy; together, he and I drove to Toledo to be with our loved ones.

~~~

I drove to Toledo like a bat flying straight from the gates of Hell. Mama was having her surgery at seven o'clock in the morning. I had to get to her before they performed surgery. I arrived at Toledo Hospital at six-thirty. I hurriedly walked through the hospital until I located the area where the operation was taking place. Many of my family members were congregated in the waiting room when I arrived.

Moments later, two doors swung open with a silver-haired lady lying on a gurney. She looked small and fragile on the bed. I walked to her, unsure of what to do or say. A tube was attached to her arm intravenously. I knelt down to hug and to kiss her.

"I love you," I said passionately.

"I love you, too, baby," Mama replied in a small voice.

Her eyes began to tear. She looked around the room at her family gathered around her. Tears trickled down her cheeks.

"What's wrong, Mama?!" Everyone asked nearly at once.

"Aww, I don't know. I guess, I'm just glad to see all of y'all here."

~~~~

After Mama was taken into the operating room, I went to Mother's house to check on her. I stepped into the house and walked through the living room into the dining room where she laid on a gurney that had been provided by hospice. Although I had lost two family members already, I was not yet familiar with the process of death. It would be years before I would fully understand the significance of hospice and what their services wholly meant.

The hospital bed looked massive in the room. Like Mama, Mother appeared small and fragile. She raised her head as I walked across the creaky floorboards.

"Hi, grandmother," I said tenderly.

She squinted her eyes in the dim light.

"Chris?" Adjusting her eyes more, "Hey, doll."

She was merely a shell of her former self. My fear had materialized. *Where was the plump, stout woman with the contagious humor?* The illness had aged her in just the few short months since I had last seen her. Her face was gaunt: the skin sagged in places where it was once firm, which was made even more apparent without her dentures in her mouth.

I walked nearer to the bed. "Hi." I smiled as I leaned down to kiss her on the forehead.

"When'd you get here?" She asked, covering her mouth with her hand.

I reached for her other hand, caressing it gently. 'Boy, yo' hands look like mine!' She had exclaimed years ago as she noticed the huge knuckles of my hands.

"I got here a couple of hours ago. Mama, my other grandmother, is in the hospital. She has cancer," I said forlornly.

"Naw!" She said raising her head from her pillow. "I'm sorry to hear that. Be sure to tell Lawanda and your family, I'ma say a prayer for them," Mother replied genuinely.

She was a remarkable lady. She had been loving and caring for people for so long that it was ingrained in her spirit to nurture. During her own time of need and prayer, she was sending prayers up to the Maker for someone else.

"Okay. I will," I smiled. "I'm going upstairs to take a nap. I'll be up in a few hours to check on you. I love you, hear?" I asked as I lightly massaged her head. She loved for her scalp to be touched.

"I love you," she replied, sweetly.

Mama's surgery had gone well. She did not have stomach cancer as Geneva had told me. Instead, she had pancreatic cancer; one of the deadliest and most aggressive of all cancers. The doctors had removed huge portions of her diseased colon to sustain her life. She was placed in a drug induced coma to aid her body in recovering sooner.

My life seemed like a living nightmare. I could not imagine anyone else enduring so much pain and suffering in such a short time span. I had no understanding as to what was going on in my life. I looked down at Mama lying virtually lifeless on the hospital bed. Her head was tilted backwards. Her mouth was agape and filled with some sort of breathing apparatus. Machines chimed indiscriminately throughout the room.

"Grandmama, this is Chris. I'm here. I don't know if you remember, but I came back home from California…I love you."

I looked down at her swollen face. Surely, this could not be my life. This could not be my grandmother lying on the bed motionless.

"Grandmama, you've got to get better. We need you. I need you. You still have to see Karisa get married and have children," I said encouragingly in reference to my younger cousin.

I bobbed and weaved through the machinery until I was able to touch her hair. The soft, silver curls shimmered radiantly under the lights. I gently stroked her hair with my hands until it looked as though it had been combed. Mama was very particular about how her hair looked.

Over the next couple of days, I alternated my time between sitting beside Mama in the hospital and spending time with Mother at home. I felt like a missionary visiting the sick and shut-in.

After showering and dressing for the day's routine, I walked into the dining room to chit-chat with Mother before I went to the hospital to visit with Mama. Mother was in a cantankerous mood. Casha, my cousin, was having a difficult time getting her to take her medication.

"I don't want it!" Mother hissed at Casha.

"Mother, what's wrong?" I asked gently as I entered the dining room.

"She's being stubborn…don't want to take her medication. Lady, you are going to take this medication!" Casha said playfully taunting Mother, as she walked in the direction of the kitchen.

"Hmm, let me see," I said motioning toward the cup of medication in Casha's hand. "Mother," I said turning to her. "You know, you have to take your medication. It'll make you feel better," I said coaxingly.

She looked at me unconvincingly, with remnants of anger still apparent on her face. I took off my jacket and set it down on a chair. It looked like I would be there for awhile. When Mother had her mind set, there was little hope of deterring her.

I went into the den and began taking family photos down from the wall.

"Mother, who is this?" I asked, showing her a photo.

She looked at the photo for a long moment before responding.

"I don't know," she replied resolutely.

I looked at her. "This is Uncle Matthew; your brother."

Uncle Matthew was Mother's oldest sibling. They had lived together for years.

"I know who my brother is, but that ain't him," She replied obstinately.

I retrieved photo after photo from the den. Some of the faces she remembered, others she did not. I was surprised. Although Mother was stricken with Alzheimer's, much of her long term memory was acute. Something was amiss.

"Mother, who is this?" I asked, showing her another photo.

She raised her head to look into the face of the woman. She looked long and hard before she finally acquiesced.

"I don't know her."

"That's you, Mother," I said gently.

She lifted her head again to look at the photo, again. "Mm mhm, no, it ain't," she said before resting her head on the pillow.

"Mother, do you know who I am?" I asked.

"No," she replied definitively.

"I'm Chris." She raised her head again as though I reminded her of someone. "Your grandson. I'm your son's son."

Her brow furrowed; her eyes became intense. She grabbed my

hand quickly and firmly.

"Are ya?" She asked, almost pleadingly.

I smiled a bit uneasily, "Yes, I am."

She held my hand with the strength of a black bear. Something was going on, but I was unsure of exactly what. She was not the same person that was lying down a few seconds ago.

"Are ya really?"

"Yes, ma'am. I am."

"I love ya! Ya hear me?! I love ya!" She said passionately.

I smiled, "I love you, too.

For several minutes into an hour, Mother and I talked. Sometimes she knew who I was; at other times, she did not. At times, she recognized our beloved family members in the photos; at times, she did not.

Finally, after nearly two hours, I was able to get her to take her medication. She rose from the pillow, threw her head back, and, with the help of some water, she swallowed the pills. As she began to lie back, she suddenly raised her head and peered into nothingness. Her countenance began to hold several different expressions in rapid succession of one another. The first look appeared to be curiosity; another looked to be fear; the other seemed to be shock.

After seeing whatever, or whomever, she saw, she laid back onto the pillow. Her eyes became translucent; peacefulness exuded from her face. I looked in the direction in which she had been staring. I saw nothing.

"Are you okay, Mother?" I asked.

She did not respond to me. She simply looked at me. I kissed her on the forehead.

"Cash, I'm going up to the hospital to check on Mama," I yelled from the dining room. "Mother, took her medication."

"Okay," she yelled from the kitchen.

I walk-ran to my car. For some reason, I was anxious to see Mama. As I entered her hospital room, everything was the same as it was when I saw her earlier that morning. I stood by her bedside talking to her; telling her how much I loved and missed her.

My cell phone rang. I was surprised. I thought I had turned off my phone. I looked down at the caller identification. Brandy.

"Hey, Bran!"

"Luda, Mother…" I began to lose reception.

"Huh? I can't understand you." I yelled into the phone.

"Mother's gone," she whimpered.

"Okay…I'm on the way back to the house," I said calmly.

I disconnected the call and turned toward Mama's bed.

"Grandmama, Mother is gone. She passed away." Tears began to stream down my face. "I forgot to tell you that she asked about you the other day. She wanted y'all to know that she was praying for you. I love you." I said as I knelt down to kiss her on the forehead before departing the room.

After Mother's funeral, I left Toledo for Atlanta. I did not know my next plan. Life, however, was not yet finished throwing blows at me. A week after my return to the city, my car was repossessed. I had not been able to secure any employment as I had expected upon my return from California. I had nearly depleted all of my savings. Without an income, I was unable to make payments on the car.

"Chris, I'm sorry your car was taken." Tiana said sincerely. Her sentiments touched my heart. "I don't think it's funny, like daddy and Tatiyanna. They just couldn't stop laughing about it, but I think it's mean of them. And, if you ever want to drive my car, you can."

I smiled as I hugged Tiana, "Thank you." I said appreciatively.

As I watched my younger sister walk away, my heart was filled with deep emotion. Her own life had not been a crystal staircase, yet, in spite of the disappointments and heartaches of her own young life, at nineteen years old, she had matured into a remarkably kind and compassionate young woman.

Even when things seem to be at their worst, God is always near showing His love and care of us. Mally had recently moved to Atlanta. After nearly three years of separation, he and I reconnected as though we had only been apart for a day. Just as before, my friendship with Mally was invaluable. I needed to be around someone whose love of me was as wholesome as his. Although, it was difficult not having the autonomy in which I had grown accustomed to with having my own vehicle, I had no choice but to deal with my circumstances. I had come to accept the loss of my transportation with ease.

For several days after my car had been repossessed, I stayed with Mally at his apartment. While he was away at work, I used my alone time to contemplate what I would do to get my life back on track now that I was back on the other side of the coast. I had lost nearly everything it seemed: one grandmother was gone; another was hanging onto life by a thread; I had no car, no job, and no home of my own.

~~~

New Year's Eve had arrived. Yet, I was not in a festive mood. Insistently, Mally had urged me to join him and his friend to bring in the New Year at one of Atlanta's popular gay clubs. I declined. A club was the very last place where I wanted to be on New Year's Day.

It was time that I fulfilled the Creator's will. His voice echoed ever so clearly in my ear, *'Tell your story,'* He admonished.

I sat for a long moment in silence. *Life's lessons.* I thought of all that I had experienced over the past fifteen years. I remembered the swooshing sound of the bullet as it exited the gun, fatally killing Adam; I recalled each agonizing year in prison; I thought of all the pain and disappointment I had experienced during the seven years that I had been home from prison.

I shook my head in disbelief. I would have never thought that life beyond bars would be so obstreperous. My life was very different than the life I had before I was incarcerated. My familial relationships were different; I had lost friends; I had acquired loved and abandoned love. Sitting in the phone room of Lima Correctional Institution with the phone cradled snuggly to my ear, Tyler's declaration rang loudly, 'Man, it's fucked up out here! You'll see, man! Home ain't home no mo'!'

I smiled a little to myself, as I thought of his prophetic words. Tyler and I had imagined home to be much different than what we had experienced after our release from prison. As inmates, we thought home was the answer to our prayers.

He Told Me. I could not deny that I had been forewarned. I had experienced life: the good, the bad, and the indifferent.

Yet, while my life was nowhere near the dream that I had envisioned it to be, I still had an opportunity to change the course of my life. I was no longer caged behind steels bars and barbed wired fencing. I was not dead. I had the hope of another day.

I breathed in deeply, welcoming the promise of a new day, as I exhaled the hurt of yesteryears. It was time. With the urging of the Holy Spirit, I followed His direction. Pushing the power button, I patiently waited for Mally's laptop computer to load and for a blank word document to appear on the screen.

With the ease of a soaring eagle, my fingers moved deftly across the keyboard of the computer, my purpose solidified, I began writing:

"Come on, Ms. Leslie! Girl, you are always the last to get dressed," Erin chided. "Girl, by the time you get all dolled up, the carnival will be over, and we woulda missed all the boys, honey!" Erin said, disapprovingly.

The End

www.ingramcontent.com/pod-product-compliance
Lightning Source LLC
Chambersburg PA
CBHW050626300426
44112CB00012B/1683